PENGUIN BOOKS

GRADING THE TEACHER

Nellie Jacobs began her career as a teacher in 1967 in the public school system. While raising her four children, her growing awareness of what it means to be a parent led her to devote more and more of her time to parenting issues. She was co-founder of the non-profit organization MAMMA (Modern Activities for Mothers' Mental Awareness) and acted as editor and publisher of its internationally received newsletter.

Grading the
TEACHER

A CANADIAN
PARENT'S GUIDE

Nellie Jacobs

Penguin Books

PENGUIN BOOKS

Published by the Penguin Group

Penguin Books Canada Ltd, 10 Alcorn Avenue, Toronto, Ontario,
Canada M4V 3B2
Penguin Books Ltd, 27 Wrights Lane, London W8 5TZ, England
Penguin Books USA Inc., 375 Hudson Street, New York,
New York 10014, U.S.A.
Penguin Books Australia Ltd, Ringwood, Victoria, Australia
Penguin Books (NZ) Ltd, 182-190 Wairau Road, Auckland 10,
New Zealand

Penguin Books Ltd, Registered Offices: Harmondsworth,
Middlesex, England

First published 1996

3 5 7 9 10 8 6 4 2

Manufactured in Canada

Canadian Cataloguing in Publication Data

Jacobs, Nellie, 1946-
Grading the teacher

ISBN0-14-025612-1

1. Teaching - Evaluation. 2. Teachers - Rating of. 3. Education -
Evaluation. 4. Education - Parent participation. I. Title.

LB1027.J33 1996   371.1'44   C95-932317-1

I dedicate Grading the Teacher *to all fine educators,
and include among those my children—
Jordan, Andrea, Ricky, and Jonathan—
whose school experiences and demands for quality
teachers motivated me to write this book.*

I've come to the frightening conclusion that I am the decisive element in the classroom. My personal approach creates the climate. My daily mood makes the weather. As a teacher, I possess tremendous power to make a child's life miserable or joyous. I can be the tool of torture or an instrument of inspiration. I can humiliate or humour, hurt or heal. In all situations, it is my response that decides whether a crisis will be escalated or de-escalated and a child humanized or de-humanized.

—Haim Ginott,
teacher, psychotherapist, writer

Acknowledgments

In recent years, I have taken numerous courses, taught by inspiring professionals who were most generous in dispensing their considerable knowledge. In keeping with the premise of this book, that we acknowledge our great teachers, I must take this opportunity to give thanks to: Elaine Clarfield-Gitalis (painting in watermedia), Ken Danziger (screenwriting), Susan Dobson (photography), Linda Griffiths (playwriting), and Barbara Turner-Vessalego (freefall creative writing). On returning to studies in the mid 1980s at the Glendon campus of York University, I was lucky to have had skilful, dedicated professors such as: Grace Jolly (an appreciation of the English language and effective writing), Peter Kolyznik (line and form in art); Ann Mackenzie (Modes of Reasoning, a course in clear and logical thinking); Baṇuta Rubess, a most original actress, director, playwright, and Rhodes scholar (theatre and playwriting); and the enormously magnanimous, internationally distinguished poet, the late bp nichol (creative writing).

I also thank the following individuals for their help, inspiration and advice: Barbara Anthony, Bill Belfontaine, Eileen Berg, Karen Fraser, Amy Goldberger, Susie Ioannidou, Elvina Heemskirk, Howie and Chris Jacobs, Zoe Kessler, Susan Leiberman, Marilyn Linton, Sandy Tobias Offenheim, Shelly Pinx, Rose Reisman, Gerry and Sherry Riskin, Dr. Gary Shomair, Jude Soosaipillai, Barbara Stein, Dr. Gitta Tafler, Ellie Tesher, and Cheryl Zaccaro.

Thanks to everyone who so generously gave their time and experience in responding to questionnaires and interviews. Some of those people are mentioned or quoted in the text of the book; others include the following: Bob Bronk, Christie Laidlaw Evans, Brian D. Harrison (Principal, Bench Elementary School, Mill Bay, British Columbia), Gary Hatcher (Director of School Services, Department of Education and Training, Newfoundland), Alexandra S. Hildebrandt (Alberta Education), Dr. Gary Hunt (Chair, Elementary Education, Faculty of Education, University of Toronto), Dr. Louisa M. Kosey (Assistant Dean and Professor,

Faculty of Education, University of Regina), Virginia MacCarthy (Faculty of Education, Malaspina University College, Nanaimo, British Columbia), Brian Menton (Director of Curriculum Services, Education, Culture and Employment, Northwest Territories), Dennis Searle (Associate Dean, Faculty of Education, York University), Diane Symes, Ralph Wightman (Quebec Provincial Association of Catholic Teachers), and the many others who preferred to remain anonymous. Special thanks to Tami Jacobs Kligman and Bill Pickering.

I offer heartfelt appreciation to my parents, Sam and Eva Waxman, to my mother-in-law, Ethel Jacobs, and to my late father-in-law Morris Jacobs, each of whose devotion sustained me in many ways through the years, and to my husband Paul, whose love and example encourage me to explore the creative world of ideas.

I wish to acknowledge my patient editors: my thanks to Meg Masters at Penguin Books for understanding what I wanted to say and who, along with Jennifer Glossop, helped focus and shape the message.

Table of Contents

Introduction

Schools are being called to account. It's about time. [They] are among the most exclusive, secretive and authoritarian power structures we will ever encounter. Parents are seldom told what their children are being taught, why or how: we have almost no ability to criticize the curriculum, evaluate the teachers or assess the schools' standards. We accept on faith. Why?[1]

—Heather Robertson

In the past, adults were expected to respect the educational system unconditionally. As a result, parents were reluctant to consider, never mind to judge, the competence of their children's teachers. Even raising questions, they feared, might be construed as criticism. In addition, many worried that they were neither educated enough to understand what was going on in the class nor articulate enough to say anything when problems arose. As a result, some children suffered incompetent or abusive teachers, and many were affected by an inflexible bureaucracy that was either

reluctant or slow to acknowledge problems.

Today, people are more aware of their rights in education. Television, radio, newspapers, and magazines regularly feature schooling issues. As well, many provincial ministries of education have gone so far as to legislate parental involvement in schools and in education policy development. More and more schools are opening their doors to parents' input and participation beyond fund-raising and classroom volunteering. Yet, in a poll published by *Parents* magazine,[2] it was discovered that even modern parents are reluctant to discuss a problem with their children's teachers. Although generally better educated and more aware of educational concerns than their own parents, today's parents still believe that they cannot appropriately deal with teachers and that any level of interference might negatively affect the teacher-child relationship.

If today's parents want to know how to deal with teachers, then they need to acknowledge the significance of the teacher's influence on their children. They need to acknowledge the importance of facing and treating school problems at their onset, before they fester and give rise to consequences that are too difficult to deal with. They also need to acknowledge each student's absolute right to be safe and nourished in an optimum learning environment.

Children enter their first year of school naive, spontaneous, fresh, and eager to learn. That year, often kindergarten, is the first of many "gardens," or classes, children encounter on the pathway of learning. What happens along the way can affect them forever. Certain teachers and experiences will leave a lifelong legacy. For some students, that inheritance will be particularly positive; for others, it will be absolutely destructive.

Unfortunately, too often students feel teachers are uncaring. One middle-aged friend will never forget her experience in grade five. Her teacher divided the students' desks into five rows titled Kings, Queens, Jacks, Bishops, and Cabbages. The pupils were assigned seats in the rows according to their performance, the Kings being the highest and the Cabbages the lowest, with status within the row itself also determined by grades. My friend sat in the centre of the Queen row and says she will never, ever forget—and it is now more than thirty-five years later—the humiliation she felt when the teacher forced her to exchange desks partway through the year with someone who'd been sitting in the Bishops row. But she didn't dare complain, because in those days students and their parents (if they even believed their children) just didn't kick up a fuss. Both felt powerless in the face of the teacher's authority.

If parents today recognize the effect teachers have on their children, why are so many intimidated by the idea of evaluating educators? Some parents feel they don't have the skills or experience. Some would prefer to leave the task to the "experts" in education. Often parents consider their concerns isolated cases—exceptions to the common experience that wouldn't be attended to. Many others believe that any attempt to change the status quo is a hopeless undertaking.

Some parents and students do, indeed, raise questions, but frequently the way they go about it is ineffective. Their outspokenness is interpreted as provoking and inciting; they are seen as too demanding or ignorant of the system and its process. The ears they reach may be either deaf or defensive. These parents get antagonistic rather than sympathetic responses.

To be effective, parents need to educate themselves, to refine their understanding of the teacher's positive and negative qualities, of the goals and the overall quality of programs and lessons. In addition, they should be sensitive to the system and its processes. Parents can learn to approach the teachers and administrators effectively at any level. Even if they can't actually check references and make decisions about hiring, parents *can* develop methods of assessing teachers in order to offer feedback, to the teachers and to the administration, and thus have some say in the calibre of their children's instructors.

A child who is having difficulty with a classroom teacher or who is faced with a cold, unresponsive school environment needs to know that someone is supportive of and sympathetic to him. Children might know if a teacher is "really good" or "really bad," but they might not know why. And if, in fact, they *do* identify what is good or bad, they don't necessarily know what to do with that information. Therefore, I urge parents to become the prime advocates for their children. By guiding their children with their own accumulated knowledge and experience, and by teaching them how to develop strategies for dealing with and working towards solving troublesome situations as they occur, parents can encourage the children to become self-confident and independent. Not only should parents be ready and equipped to defend their kids if the need arises, they should also be prepared to work with the teachers to help their children.

Grading the Teacher was inspired by my own first-hand observations. Five years of teaching in elementary schools gave me the chance to get some insider information on the education system, and my later experience as the mother of four children allowed me to look at it from the other side, from the parent's perspective. Among them, at various times, my children attended public, private, and alternative schools and were enrolled in a variety of different programs—language immersion, gifted, and special needs. At one point, I had a child in each level of the school system: one in elementary school, one in junior high, one in high school, and the eldest attending university. Through my own experiences and those of my friends and acquaintances, many of whom were educators themselves, I discovered that many teachers and parents were unable to act effectively in the best interests of the children. Eventually I went back to school myself to take further university courses, and I found myself evaluating my instructors: were they helpful, effective, inspiring? What made the difference between a good teacher and a poor one?

When I sat down to write, I had several goals in

mind. *Grading the Teacher* is about accountability and empowerment. It's about stepping back to assess the educational system, public or private, beginning with the classroom. It's about evaluating the classroom teacher, who ultimately represents that system and who, of all the professionals involved in education, has the greatest impact on our children. It's also about the fact that those individuals in administration who set policies, strategies, and short- and long-term goals are no less responsible for the well-being and success of our children than the classroom teacher.

The book proposes a twist on the classroom evaluation: here, teachers will be appraised by the pupils and their parents. In the following chapters I will examine the criteria by which parents can judge individual teachers' performance. A detailed report card is included which can be used to "grade the teacher," or just to suggest the issues and questions that parents might want to address.

Validating concerns about the quality of their children's teachers, the book gives a frame of reference and backup support to *all* parents, not just those whose kids are having problems at school. This book is not intended as a diatribe against teachers. The majority of teachers are very good at what they do; some are excellent. If parents don't already appreciate who these good teachers are, the material within these pages should help to identify them. It should reinforce the opinions of parents who are, in fact, pleased with their child's educational experience but perhaps don't trust their own judgment. However, this information also shows parents how to recognize teachers' weaknesses and inefficiencies and offers strategies for bringing them to the teachers' or administration's attention. It guides parents in productively approaching their children's educators for help and offers suggestions for solutions to problems they might encounter along the way. In addition, it includes insights as to how a "system" works, so that parents can apply that knowledge to their own school situations. By removing the sense of isolation parents feel when they approach educational institutions, *Grading the Teacher* empowers parents, encouraging them to articulate their anxieties or questions.

As a parent, you are the person most in tune with your child's needs and stages of development; if you think something is wrong or lacking at school, strive for change. Learn to recognize problems in the classroom. Learn to recognize both the positive and the negative qualities of teachers. Learn how the system works, what questions to ask in order to help the student, and how to work with the teacher to make improvements. As a parent of a school-age child you have a right to be concerned; there are things to be concerned about.

Try, however, to be concerned in a positive way. By educating yourself and by learning constructive approaches, you *can* make a difference in the quality of your child's education. Yes, you can work towards educating the educators. Moreover, by identifying and acknowledging those individuals who are outstanding,

nurturing teachers, you can reward them and, at the same time, work towards informing and helping teachers who need to improve.

Notes on Terminology

Certain nomenclature is interchangeable, depending on the school and its district. For example, the "principal" is usually the person who heads a single school administration. However, some school systems, whether they are private or public, may refer to this person as "headmaster/mistress" or "director/directrice," among other titles. "Department heads" are found in high schools and some junior highs; they supervise the teachers and course expectations within a particular discipline such as English, Drama, Science, or Math.

When I first started teaching, "inspector" was the designation given to administrators responsible for several schools in their district[3]; the term now used is "superintendent." In managing a block of schools, superintendents ensure a liaison between those schools and their board of education. "Directors of education" are appointed to run each board, somewhat like the company president or chief executive officer.

Generally, the term "administrator" includes, among others, principals, vice-principals, headmasters, department heads, superintendents, and directors of education. For the most part, these people are teachers who advanced through the hierarchy and qualified for their positions by fulfilling particular pre-established criteria,

which may have included a certain length of tenure, specific areas of expertise and experience, as well as completion of numerous courses and degrees.

Private schools often stand entirely on their own with no other hierarchy. The main administrator— whether principal, headmaster, or director—may be the founder of the school, his or her heir, or someone hired by the board of directors, by the owner of the school, or by the parents. Although the standards of the school can be established by any or all of these individuals or groups, the chief administrator is generally answerable to no one but him or herself.

If the labels you encounter are different from those I use, ask the teacher, principal, or office staff at your child's school to explain their terminology.

Chains of Authority

1. STANDARD ELEMENTARY SCHOOL:

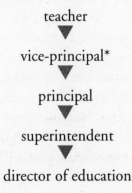

teacher
▼
vice-principal*
▼
principal
▼
superintendent
▼
director of education

2. STANDARD JUNIOR HIGH SCHOOL/HIGH SCHOOL:

teacher

▼

staff adviser/guidance counsellor

▼

department head

▼

vice-principal*

▼

principal

▼

superintendent

▼

director of education

3. PRIVATE SCHOOL:

teacher

▼

principal/headmaster/director

▼

school proprietor *

▼

board of directors *

▼

parents *

* May or may not exist or be part of the chain

CHAPTER ONE

A Good School

*Schools flourish when they have community sup-
port, parental involvement, devoted teachers
with a zest for the task, and when they offer
emotional nurturance for "at risk" students.*[1]
—Michelle Landsberg

The good school plays many roles. Its program of
studies is challenging, progressive, current, and
individualized. It provides an environment that is
peaceful, safe, positive, and nurturing. It guarantees to
each child a caring teacher and to each teacher a program of support and professional guidance.

To judge the excellence of a school, there are a number of factors to consider. This chapter emphasizes
those I regard as essential. They are classified under two
major areas: the school's policies and its resources.

GRADING THE TEACHER

Policies

A good school cultivates policies that are clear, evident, and well communicated. In *If Learning Is So Natural, Why Am I Going to School?*, author Andrew Nikiforuk writes that a good school can:

> ...typically explain in clear language what its program is, what it expects in academic and behavioural performance, what happens to those who succeed or fail and how changes in performance are monitored.
>
> It evaluates all programs on the basis of pupil achievement and reports progress or lack of it regularly, honestly and meaningfully. Effective schools not only tell parents when children are experiencing difficulty, they forward a plan of action.[2]

Knowing exactly where it wants to go and how to get there allows a school to fully develop its potential. It accomplishes this end partly by creating a mission statement (or mandate) and a set of goals. This process should involve the careful consideration of the administration and input from any combination of staff, students, and parents.

1. Mission Statement

A mission statement is a general declaration of overarching principles and goals. An example of such a statement is the one embraced by the North York Board of Education: "To empower every student to learn to achieve success and to participate responsibly in a pluralistic global society."

Does your school, board, or district have a mission statement? Ask the principal. If a mission statement does exist, what is it? Who wrote it—administrators, staff, students, and/or parents? Do you consider it feasible, reasonable, and timely? Sometimes mission statements look good on paper but are so generalized that it is difficult to assess their usefulness. Does the mission statement reflect your own ideas about education? Do the teachers know what it is? Ask them. What is being done to implement it? Try to find parents, teachers, or administrators who will tell you if it is truly adhered to.

2. Goals

The mission statement is a philosophical expression of lofty goals. To realize the mandate's fullest hope, each school should also articulate specific aims and objectives that are relevant and timely. Ask about the school's immediate and long-range goals. Are they well defined? How appropriate are they for the times? Do they meet the students' needs? Do they meet the community's needs? Do they help prepare students for an independent and successful future?

The short- and long-term goals of one Winnipeg high school acknowledge the necessity of keeping pace with a changing world. The school's short-term goals are: "mentoring" for teacher growth—a program in which experienced teachers help others along by support and example; introduction of Asian-Pacific studies; reorganization for improved communication within the school and between the school and parents; and increased power for students, parents, and staff. The long-term plans are: the addition of grade nine to the existing grades ten to twelve; to become technologically relevant; and to increase school-community-business partnership.

Both short- and long-term objectives were developed together with staff, students, parents, and local business, with the approval of the superintendent. They were then communicated to the general school community through mailings, meetings, and local media. These goals reflect a recognition that teachers helping their peers create not only better teachers but also a more positive working environment. In addition, through the development of Asian-Pacific studies, the school recognizes its changing demographics and worldwide influences.

What can you do if a clear mandate doesn't exist at your school, or if it is no longer relevant, if goals are nonexistent or if they are poorly defined? If you already have an idea, you might propose to the administration and to the school's parents' association (if there is one) that you are prepared to work with them towards helping develop new mandates and/or goals.

School Resources

A school's resources include not only its physical environment and its equipment but also the teaching and administrative staff, the office personnel, the community at large, and the extra-curricular activities. The quality of resources and how they are used reflects on the quality of the school.

1. Physical environment and equipment

In researching a school's resources, you can note if school equipment and supplies are adequate. Are they maintained regularly and replaced when necessary? Look at the physical layout of the school and its environment: do they encourage learning? For example, certain open-plan schools have no walls separating the classes; these schools might not be suitable for students whose attention is easily diverted. Some schools might not have windows in classrooms, a predicament that could cause problems for those who are claustrophobic or who have allergies. Keep in mind, however, that good teaching and learning can take place in many situations. Don't be persuaded by external factors alone.

2. Staff/Administration

A good school ensures that its staff members are well qualified, enthusiastic, and caring. In fact, the greatest resource a school has is its teaching staff. The eagerness of the teachers can greatly encourage school spirit and student participation. A good school draws to it and holds teachers who are individually and collectively enthusiastic. They support each other, willingly pool their resources, and share ideas and information. Because they know it is for the collective good, the teachers, as well as their administrators, inspire and encourage each other to do well and to better themselves. To these ends, a good school should have in place teacher support systems, such as an effective mentoring program.

The teachers in a good school are self-analytical, constantly searching for ways to improve their skills. At regular get-togethers for reflection and brainstorming, each member of the teaching staff welcomes suggestions for improvement. Encouraged by their superiors, a good school's teachers are motivated to keep up with changing times by taking upgrading courses.

Finally, in a good school both staff and administrators recognize that each person and department is a valuable aspect of the entire infrastructure. As in any working environment, each person needs to feel that his efforts are important, recognized, and that he is part of a valued team. The process of working together as a team provides not only a supportive, cohesive unit for the school professionals but the best kind of support and learning environment for the students. In a case where a student, for example, has a personal problem such as an illness or death in the family, or where he needs special help with a particular skill, all his teachers and the school administration would be notified and advised how to handle it. They might sit down together to assess

the situation and what they could do to improve it.

3. Office staff

How else can you judge if a school is good? In my experience, one of the best "windows" to the school is its office staff. It is their role to expedite certain concerns before they go through administration. They can identify problems as they happen and put solutions in motion.

While visiting the office, stand aside and notice the way office personnel responds to its teaching staff and how it handles the students. Are the people staffing the office pleasant? Do they respond to issues or questions professionally and efficiently? Do they pay attention to each individual, whether staff, student, parent, or "outsider"? Do they respond positively to every request and task? How "student friendly" is the office staff? Do they deal with questions and concerns with care and interest? Does the "buck stop here"? Or is the person seeking help ignored altogether?

In the hands of a good office staff the students and parents are welcomed and respected. If they encounter negative experiences with office personnel, students and parents might be reluctant to bring problems to official attention. They might feel they or their concerns are not considered important. Dealings with the office might also colour their attitudes towards the administration and teaching staff. As a result, they might become less willing to raise their problems at all, or to do it in an agreeable way.

4. Community Presence

Good schools work hand-in-hand with their local communities and often play a leadership role. Many schools reflect the community in transition. A good school adapts itself to deal with new demands, such as a changing ethnic mix or increasingly troubled economic and social circumstances in the neighbourhood. For example, a school's professional development days might feature workshop leaders who can enlighten teaching staff and administration by defining those changes, sensitize the educators to the community difficulties, and arm them with techniques to deal with the results.

A good school tries to provide support services and programs that involve not only the school community at large but also individual students and their families. It welcomes students to participate in any projects researching their own ethnicity or that of their families and encourages them to share their discoveries with their classmates. It invites parents into the class to teach about their cultures or histories, their jobs or hobbies. An ideal school welcomes and encourages community participation.

A good school draws upon the talents and skills of its community. Are students, parents, local professionals, business people, and politicians invited to develop and participate in relevant programs? Are they asked, for example, to come into the school to take part in career days? Are days set aside for students to visit their parents' work and report back to their class about the experience?

Parents and other community members can help staff develop school policies, as well as plan and participate in special school programs such as fund-raisers or full-day workshops. Find out if and how parents are welcomed into the school. Is there a parents' association or parents' council? Many provincial ministries of education across Canada are mandating this kind of involvement in public schools. If there is such a group, what is its focus? Does it reflect your own concerns?

Even private schools don't always issue a blanket welcome to parents. For example, Crestwood School has a parents' association, and as director Dalia Eisen points out, "Parents can be as much or as little involved as they want to be." But, she underlines, the role of the association is basically fund-raising for extra equipment such as computers. On the other hand, the Winnipeg high school mentioned earlier welcomes parents' involvement with staff and administration through committees on relevant topics; as participants in focus groups that analyze and resolve special school-related issues, such a multiculturalism and racism or the need to raise funds for up-to-date equipment; by taking advantage of their expertise at the school in shared services offered to staff and students; and by encouraging volunteers on the parent- and student-advisory committee.

5. Extra-curricular Activities

Pay attention to the extra-curricular activities, like sports and clubs, that the school offers. If they do exist, how dynamic, diverse, and suitable to the interests of

the students are they? Are they well attended? Are they designed so that your child can easily participate? For example, young students who travel long distances by car pool or by public transportation to their school often cannot be involved in after-school clubs or pro- grams. If the school has many students in such a situa- tion, the staff might offer special activities at lunchtime. All of these extra-curricular activities influence the camaraderie and spirit of the staff and students.

How to Judge a School

Now that you know what to look for, how do you go about getting the information that you need? Schools often have a reputation within as well as outside their community. In addition to their local students, the very best schools usually develop waiting lists for students living out of the area. To gather your own information, listen to as many perceptions and opinions of the school as you can.

There are several ways to go about collecting input about a school. Attend community meetings about education. Speak to as many students as you can. Contact their parents. Ask both to recommend others. Speak with your local trustee. Meet with the school administrator(s). The office staff of the school can also be helpful, but if you ask for references keep in mind that the school will most likely direct you to model students or families supportive of the school. Go beyond that. Try to find the "ordinary" students and their families. Neighbours who have school-age children will usually give you *plenty* of information. Although it might be difficult to find them—and if you do they might be reluctant to jeopardize their jobs by saying too much—supply teachers can give you a great deal of insight into the quality of the school and its staff. Any experienced supply teacher needs only a day in a teacher's class to know the teacher's structure, routine, and priorities.

When judging schools, look at the attributes of a good school mentioned in this chapter and consider their importance to you. Few schools will score high in all areas. If a school doesn't have a state-of-the-art computer system, or if its office staff is unfriendly, or if it must use the local park or YMCA facilities since the school lacks a gymnasium, do not immediately conclude that the school is not good or has no value to your child. Decide what is best for your child's needs, and be mindful of the school's benefits, such as its proximity to your home, its great music program, or its enthusiastic teaching staff. Weighing the positives and the negatives carefully, keep in mind your own expectations and your child's needs. But also remember that the greatest influence on the child can be the quality of the teacher himself.

CHAPTER TWO

Recognizing Good Teaching

Teaching, as I see it, is the noblest of professions. Fine teachers...care about their subjects so much that their students are "caught" by their enthusiasm.[1]

—Fred Rogers

The general purpose or mandate of a teacher is to impart knowledge. But there is more to teaching than just passing on information. The teacher can use his curriculum and the information he teaches to facilitate and co-ordinate the development of the student. The teacher can help the student mature, not just by passing on knowledge and skills but also by encouraging personal growth.

There are two very special gifts that a good teacher strives to bestow on every student. The first is a thirst for knowledge. Through her own excitement about learning as well as her stimulating lessons, the teacher whets the student's appetite for education. The teacher's second gift, perhaps the greatest of all, is confidence—confidence to explore ideas and to make mistakes. A good teacher's every word and action takes into consideration its effect on each student's self-esteem.

How do teachers know they are successful? Each and every teacher has his or her own yardstick. Some teachers consider themselves successful if students are caught up in their enthusiasm about the lesson or subject. They believe that even the most boring topic can be made exciting. Others consider themselves a success if students learn from them, and if in the process they respect what the teachers are doing.

Success in the short term might be that the kids show up everyday with their work done. For some teachers there's nothing more rewarding than seeing students whose work is completed and who participate in class. For other teachers, long-term success might be that students are able to achieve what the teachers set out for them to achieve—whether it's learning a variety of new skills or acquiring certain information and knowledge—and passing with good marks, at the end of the year. For Elaine Vine, English teacher and co-ordinator of the Toronto alternative high school Interact, success means that by the end of their senior year her students can develop a thesis, read material, do the research, put a paper together, and write it. Further success is indicated by the ability to read and analyze a piece of literature on their own, and to apply the critical thinking and problem-solving skills that she and her fellow teachers have taught them. "If they can make it in the outside world, then the students are successful. If we haven't trained them for that, then we haven't done anything."

Many teachers thrive on the high generated by special moments of success. It is often those moments of personal feedback and satisfaction that keep those teachers going. Perhaps it comes when a student's eyes light up with sudden understanding of a difficult concept, when a spirited conversation in class indicates the students' keen interest in the subject, or when students visit after class to talk.

Teachers' successes are rarely based on how generally well liked they are. They don't universally try to win popularity contests. Indeed, the decision to become a teacher who makes a difference in someone's life usually takes little account of whether students will like them or not.

Most of the people I interviewed in preparation for this book needed little prompting to recall a special teacher who influenced them in a positive way and whose abilities and attitudes uncovered limitless positive qualities in their students. One person, for example, remembered the elementary school teacher who made math easy; another recalled the high school teacher who taught the rules of grammar so well that she will never forget them; my own grade two teacher turned me onto a lifelong love affair with reading. Like sparks, outstanding teachers light up and excite their students; they often serve as mentors who encourage their charges towards goals otherwise thought unattainable. Terrific teachers are like bright beacons, drawing to them students who become truly eager to learn.

Do not underestimate the enormous difference that one teacher can make in a student's life. In his book *Growing Up Firstborn*, Dr. Kevin Leman, an internationally known psychologist, lecturer, and popular author, recalls the impression a teacher made upon him in high school. In those days, he was "very near the bottom of my class. You didn't find my name on any honour roll lists, and you can bet all the best colleges were not beating a path to my door." One day this teacher helped him see that he'd "been playing a game with life, rolling along content to be, as she put it, 'the best at being the worst.'" Her words "stung me, primarily because I knew she was telling the truth...I knew that I had the ability to change, and I resolved that I would change."[2]

So, how do parents know if their child's teacher is good? What constitutes a fine teacher? What are the signs parents should be looking for? Good teachers demonstrate numerous common traits. This chapter will look at a list that I've compiled over two decades. Some attributes were drawn from my experiences as a teacher, noting the qualities that impressed me about outstanding colleagues. Some were added as a result of my children's school experiences and their own suggestions. Friends, relatives, and acquaintances—many of whom are also teachers—added their input. The rest of the list developed out of extensive research, including reading, personal correspondence, and interviews with educators across the country.

The traits of a good teacher specified in this chapter are considered from four perspectives: the teacher's attitude, skills, expectations, and feedback.

A. ATTITUDE

1. A good teacher loves teaching.

First and foremost, it is evident that good teachers cherish what they are doing. Their creative juices flow when they teach. I know teachers whose outstanding skills would ensure them great success in many other fields, but they would just not be content away from teaching. Without doubt, the positive attitude of an excellent teacher who dedicates herself to her career stands out. She has a freshness, a spontaneity, that tells you she thoroughly enjoys her work. How can you recognize this teacher? Her passion for teaching and her concern for her students are obvious.

2. A good teacher exhibits goodwill.

To the best of his ability, an excellent teacher maintains an optimistic frame of mind towards teaching itself and towards his students. He *wants* the students to succeed. He *wants* to address their collective and individual needs. He *aspires* to teach his students what they need to know—within the framework of the curriculum and beyond—in order to develop their best potential as well as their ability to become successfully independent. Years ago, a wonderful teacher I knew told me she considered each and every one of her students the future leaders of the country. She felt a zealous responsibility to arm those students with the skills and knowledge not only to achieve their goals but to be able to continue using and building on them for the rest of their lives.

Teachers with goodwill are those who are the most generous with their time and their knowledge, and who give freely of themselves. Generous teachers are easily and regularly accessible to their students and their students' parents for conversation and help. The teacher with goodwill is recognizable in the positive reinforcement he offers to students. He demonstrates to them how to improve their work and how to better themselves. When meeting or speaking to parents, rather than reeling off a litany of complaints about the child, he tries to balance his assessment with positive remarks. He offers to students and parents support, suggestions, and solutions to problems.

3. A good teacher is receptive.

Never ignoring either the needs of the class as a whole or those of individual students, the responsive teacher is open to talking with her students, discussing problems, and seeking solutions. She believes that one cannot teach effectively without knowing what the kids are feeling. So, if she notices inattentive, distracted, or unruly students, she will take them aside to talk. Open discussions with students can help a teacher identify not only problems but also their individual and collective levels of knowledge and understanding, so that she can take them beyond it.

A receptive teacher makes herself available. When a student requests help, the teacher offers it as soon as possible. She is quick to arrange appointments with students and parents. She also returns their telephone calls promptly. She is responsive to their needs as well as to their suggestions.

4. A good teacher is a supportive listener.

Being a good listener requires patience, compassion, sympathy, and empathy. And of course a good listener tries not to be judgmental. It's important that kids feel that someone at their school cares about them. Many supportive teachers are proud that former students still come back to visit, often to talk about new situations in their lives, at school, at home, or in a new career. By demonstrating that they are truly interested, teachers can exemplify to their students the lifelong benefit of caring for and connecting with other people.

Teachers who are supportive listeners are easily identifiable. During telephone calls or meetings they give full attention to pupils, allowing enough time for a complete and uninterrupted discussion. Supportive listeners offer the same attentiveness to parents.

5. A good teacher is patient.

A good teacher recognizes that each student comes from a different background of experience and knowledge. Knowing that each person absorbs and retains knowledge and skills at a different rate, he patiently accommodates for that difference. Welcoming all inquiries, he takes time to listen and to respond.

6. A good teacher is self-analytical.

A good teacher continually analyzes her methods, procedures, and their results. If the class's or an individual student's results are not as good as she had expected, a conscientious teacher investigates the reasons, analyzes students' problems or difficulties, decides upon the solutions, and then makes the necessary changes to improve. Although she continually weighs whether she is giving as much as she can to the individual and to the group, she also accepts the fact that she cannot totally satisfy all students' needs all the time. When it is too hard to deal with all the individual problems, she tries to gather up common difficulties to address with the class as a whole. In the end, however, she might just have to acknowledge that she cannot inspire everyone to be successful.

A good teacher who continually analyzes her teaching is self-confident enough to welcome suggestions as to how her program and/or teaching can be more effective. If parents, students, or peers identify a problem to her, she works to solve it, together with them if possible.

7. A good teacher motivates with enthusiasm.

A teacher's exuberance invariably lights up the class and becomes incredibly motivating. Students are caught up by their teacher's enthusiasm and love of learning. A stimulating teacher easily captivates those about him and extends his excitement to both students and parents. It is simple to recognize if your child is motivated by his teacher(s). If he is eager to go to school and learn, if he enjoys putting effort into projects and homework, if he shares his enthusiasm, then you know his teacher's own excitement is helping to motivate him.

8. A good teacher is honest and reliable.

Whether she wants to be one or not, a teacher knows that she often serves as a role model to her students. In all instances a good teacher is honest. She honours, for example, every appointment she makes with parents or students. She also shows up on time. Mark H. McCormack, author of What *They Don't Teach You at Harvard Business School*, contends that one of the major attributes of a professional is reliability:

> If you *say* you're going to do something, *do it*. If you can't do it, think it's more trouble than it's worth, or don't *want* to do it, then *don't say you will*."[3]

If kids don't believe that the teacher is on their side, they're never going to really learn from her. Students *know* when their teacher is being honest; they also *know* when the teacher is being patronizing. If she doesn't know the answer to a question, a good teacher will say so.

Not only is a good teacher honest, she is also trustworthy; if, for example, she says she'll give bonus grades or rewards, she gives them. Likewise, if she sets up reasonable rules and appropriate sanctions for breaking them, she follows through. If a teacher tells parents she will take a particular course of action, she does.

9. A good teacher is discreet.

I cannot emphasize enough the importance of trust and the significance of keeping confidences. A teacher is a professional. In this capacity she may receive or have access to confidential information about her students. She never divulges secrets; never is indiscreet; and never reveals students' names or private information in non-professional conversations.

10. A good teacher has a sense of humour.

An outstanding teacher understands the value of humour, and that it is absolutely essential in teaching. Humour is more than just telling jokes or being corny. It's being at ease with the students. It's being able to laugh *with* them and perhaps sharing stories related to the issues being taught. Humour provides balance and helps to keep things in perspective. It can also open a student's receptivity to difficult theories and situations. Humour relieves tensions and defuses tempers and volatile situations, as well as contributing a much-needed break in the midst of stress.

B. SKILLS

1. A good teacher communicates well.

A good teacher is articulate. She has an excellent command of the language and is able to articulate clearly her explanations and her responses to questions. "When we communicate well, we empower our kids to think and feel and problem-solve with confidence. We allow them to become fully who they are," declares MarySue McCarthy, a professor in the Faculty of Education at York University. Effective communication clarifies, simplifies, and edifies. When whole parts of information are divided into small bits, it is far easier for students to understand and thus learn the whole.

After sessions with a good teacher, students and parents walk away satisfied that they understand what the teacher said, and that she adequately and effectively answered their questions and concerns.

2. A good teacher is knowledgeable.

A good teacher is so thoroughly familiar with the topic he is teaching that he can comfortably identify the fundamentals at the beginning of the course, easily lead the students through the various stages of knowledge step by step, and effortlessly answer their questions—or at least direct them to the answers.

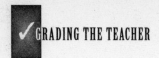

A good teacher never feels he knows enough. He is always improving his knowledge and skills. He takes courses, seminars, and workshops to acquire more ideas, to learn different methodologies, to develop his personal interests, to expand his own horizons, and to become inspired.

He regularly communicates with his associates, sharing his ideas with them, for he knows that teachers who sequester themselves and don't talk to their colleagues about the business of teaching never develop professionally. He welcomes and participates in discussions about teaching successes and difficulties. He develops strengths from new ideas and suggestions, as well as from constructive criticism.

3. A good teacher teaches relevant information.

A good teacher ensures that the subjects and lessons she is teaching are useful and relevant to the students. What motivates students to learn? Material that is interesting to them personally and relevant to the world around them. Does the teacher put her subject into context for the student? Does she show the students the usefulness of the concepts she teaches?

Visual presentations and physical interaction are often helpful in showing students, especially the younger ones, how the ideas they are being taught fit into the real world. Teachers might place their kids in roles. For instance, science teachers can have their students take on the parts of what they are studying, such as the organs of the body, or plants and animals.

History teachers often have their students dress and act according to the custom of the period they are studying. A child can be drawn into a subject through his own interests in art, science, music, drama, or any other field. Once the student is allowed to be creative he becomes involved in the learning. He'll be able to absorb facts and enjoy the process.

How can you tell if your child is in fact learning information and if so, if it's relevant? Notice if your child is applying new ideas to the world around her. Does she tell you about her newfound knowledge? Has she begun to participate in discussions using this knowledge? Keep in touch with the teacher. I once taught a shy child in kindergarten who could talk perfectly well, but was mute in the classroom for the entire first term. I knew he was learning, however, because his mother let me know that at home he sang all the songs and recited the alphabet and the numbers he had learned. He also related each day's events to her. Does your child share with you or demonstrate in any fashion what she has learned? If she doesn't talk or let you know, look at her assignments. Her new knowledge might also come out in subtle ways, in conversations or in the questions she asks. She might show extra interest in certain television or radio shows, or in reading more about a new topic.

4. A good teacher teaches study, essay-writing, and test-taking skills.

Careful development of thinking and reasoning abilities enables pupils to problem-solve, an essential skill that will serve them in all facets of their lives. Linda Miller, assistant head of the Gifted Program at Earl Haig Secondary School in North York, Ontario, says the famous question posed to her is, "When am I ever going to use this?" And she always answers,

> You're right. The distance formula will not get you a date. Socially, it's a dud. Let's get that out of the way. However, what we are really doing is we're solving a problem: we're getting a situation, we're looking at it, we're saying, "Boy, I know all these things that would help me. I know that I need to get an answer that looks sort of like this. How can I use what I know to break it down and to write it out clearly so somebody else can follow it along?" That's what I'm really teaching you.

It is critical that young students learn practical techniques, habits, and responsibilities that will serve them well in later years. Even primary students can be taught to become organized. One method involves the use of a daybook to record special dates, events, and deadlines for homework and assignments. Some schools now ensure that all students own daily planners or organizers. Teachers regularly check students' entries to verify that they are keeping it up to date. Not only do the teachers sign the books periodically, they expect parents to do so also.

Good teachers also teach their students the study, essay-writing, and test-writing skills that will lead them to success, not only in school but throughout their lives.

I. Study Skills

In addition to teaching information, a good teacher teaches students a wide variety of study and learning skills. These skills might include how to read for information, how to take notes, how to collect and arrange notes in an orderly and acceptable fashion, and how to organize and prioritize information and ideas. The teaching of these skills becomes a vital part of each assignment. In other words, he shows his students that study involves thinking clearly and logically and working in a systematic manner.

II. Essay-writing Skills

At a dinner party recently, a university student's mother asked each of the guests if they knew of anyone who had written an essay about a certain tribe of African pygmies. She was hoping to buy one for her son, whose assignment deadline was looming near. Her search, however, was in vain. Why, she moaned, did teachers give such difficult assignments and tests to poor, over-worked students? The university student's mother was not doing her son any favours by buying a paper for him. Not only was she acting as a willing and active accomplice to a fraud, she was also denying her son learning experiences and skills development that would benefit him for the rest of his life.

In addition to developing a student's responsibility, essays and projects provide him with a chance to take stock of a newly taught unit by gathering together, interpreting, collating, and applying the unit's information. It is true that these assignments supply an accumulation of marks, but they also afford the opportunity to develop organizational and problem-solving skills. Assignments and essays help students to research, to amalgamate, to apply, and, finally, to learn new information. A good teacher takes his students through a step-by-step methodology for essay-writing in order to help them achieve this important goal.

III. TEST-TAKING SKILLS

Tests provide a goal to which students can work. There are three parts to that goal: to learn the new information, to show how much of it is absorbed, and to use it in different ways.

A good teacher prepares his students in test-writing techniques. He gives them useful strategies—such as leaving a difficult question worth low marks for later. He also uses exams and tests as a teaching tool. "Teachers who only teach you answers to tests, cheat you out of an education," writes Wess Roberts, Ph.D. in *Straight A's Never Made Anybody Rich*,[4] but tests do give feedback to the teacher and to the student about how well concepts are understood, learned, remembered, and utilized. They can indicate to the teacher how effective his or her teaching has been.

For students to learn from their mistakes, they need

to know *why* their answers are wrong. The good teacher discusses marked tests with the students. If pressed for time, he can at least post the solutions at the back of the class so students can see the correct answers. To clear up misunderstandings and to review difficult ideas or concepts, good teachers discuss the answers with students either in class or privately. They also explain the criteria they use for grading. Unfortunately, some teachers use the same tests year after year; these teachers are reluctant to return tests because they don't want students in successive years to have easy access to them. Good teachers take the time to set new and better tests each year.

5. A good teacher is well organized.

One tends to take for granted that all teachers are organized and that they have specific goals. The truth of the matter is that too many choose to fly by the seat of their pants. One teacher I know decides on what he is teaching each day the moment he enters the schoolroom. Even his tests are "off the cuff," composed as he stands in front of the class.

Students, especially those in the higher grades, *know* when a teacher comes to class unprepared, and whether he is teaching a lesson of substance or just winging it. Students also resent being told to be better organized by those very educators who demonstrate no organization themselves. A teacher's organization or lack of it sets an example.

Good teachers develop efficient work habits that

measure and evenly distribute the overall workload. They cover the course over the term without either cramming or leaving out important information at the end, and they assign to the students work and projects at a pace that can be reasonably and properly dealt with by both teacher and students. This includes allowing sufficient time not only for teachers to grade work but also for its timely return to students so that it can be taken up and reviewed together while its contents and issues are still fresh in the students' minds.

As a leader and a role model for her students, a good teacher is well prepared, with lessons and assignments developed and planned beforehand. A good teacher keeps an efficient filing system for records of students' marks and papers and other documents. She regularly updates it, keeps it in order, and makes students' complete records available to parents when requested.

There are many ways that a parent can identify an organized teacher. For one thing, organized teachers generally demand that their students be organized as well. Does the teacher check notebooks and suggest how they might be improved? Is the child aware of the teacher's routines? Does the teacher prepare your child for tests by giving pre-tests or handouts explaining what will be on them? Does the child get enough advance notice about tests? In conversations and meetings, can the teacher analyze your child's progress at any point in the year? Does she have a file with your child's work, tests, and project results to which she can refer?

6. A good teacher accommodates individual needs.

A good teacher both recognizes the common needs of the class and determines the needs and interests of the individual students. He addresses those in lesson plans and assignments, focusing on the most important and the most achievable. This is one of the most difficult tasks of any teacher. As classes get larger, it becomes even more challenging for teachers to prioritize and effectively accomplish these goals.

A good teacher is flexible in his approach and in his lesson plans. He is eager to use whatever means and resources are available to him. He compromises when the situation warrants it. He understands his students' differences of knowledge and learning styles. He accepts the fact that each student brings to the learning environment a distinct set of experiences. He doesn't take for granted that his students all have the same knowledge, background, skills, or ability to learn. Attuned to his students' needs, a good teacher is always searching for new and more useful methods and examples. As a result, the good teacher changes or augments his mode of teaching when the need arises and also makes allowances for special circumstances.

Acknowledging each student's style of learning and processing information, he allows learning to take place at the rate of each individual's ability to understand, and to absorb, the information taught. How might parents know that a teacher is flexible? If they inform the teacher that their child has particular difficulty, a good teacher will actually take that information into account when dealing with the child, or the class, in the future.

A good teacher tries to be fair. Fairness and flexibility are very much tied together, because being fair sometimes means changing the playing field so that certain individuals can participate on an equal footing with everyone else. Richard D. Lavoie, hosting an excellent videotape workshop entitled *How Difficult Can This Be?*, outlines his definition of fairness: "Fairness does *not* mean that everyone gets the same. Fairness actually means that everyone gets what he or she *needs*. In order to be fair we've got to treat [each child's special needs] differently."[5]

What can you look for? When students are given assignments, does the teacher tailor them to account for individual differences? If so, are the students allowed to follow their own interests within the framework of the expectations? How does the teacher allow for creative approaches to accommodate his students' individual needs? For example, in a project on transportation, can students choose to focus on what interests them: its history, the development through the ages, a particular era, modes of transit, inventors? Are options open to them, such as art posters, an illustrated book, drama skits, and video or oral taped interviews instead of only front-of-the-class presentations. Has your child been allowed to pursue his own interests?

7. A good teacher establishes and maintains discipline.

A good teacher engenders discipline through appropriate classroom management. Without question, it is the responsibility of the teacher to ensure that a non-threatening atmosphere for learning exists. To have a successfully operating classroom, good teachers lay the groundwork with the students for their co-operation, good behaviour, and positive attitudes at the beginning of the year. This groundwork means outlining expectations of behaviour. A good teacher lets students know what behaviour is expected of them and what will not be tolerated. He follows up on infractions consistently and fairly without resorting to any unjust penalty.

Sometimes, to instil responsibility in students, it is necessary for teachers to "police" their work. For example, they may choose to regularly check assigned homework, especially with younger children. If students know from the very beginning that teachers expect the work to be done, and that it will be checked, they will do it. By defining his rules and regulations, the teacher and his students can work within their framework.

If a teacher fails to enstill discipline, childen might be hyperactive after a day at school. They *can* be overstimulated. "Creating doesn't tolerate boundaries; it demands them," declares Nita Leland in *Creative Artist.*[6] No matter how creative or avant-garde the setting, the development of any effective learning program must be within some sort of a structured framework. Spontaneity is one thing—but if a teacher doesn't run her classroom in an organized fashion, then children might not respond to her creativity. Some children need more help and instruction. Discipline that is too strict, however, can create an atmosphere of fear or resentment. Good teachers find the balance between too much discipline and too little. They know that neither a laissez-faire attitude nor an overly strict regimen generates the best learning environment for students or teachers.

What can you ask your children about classroom management? "Are the kids in the class well behaved and respectful?" "Are they and the teacher calm?" "Are there rules about behaviour?" "Is the teacher fair but consistent in the way he deals with bad behaviour?"

C. Expectations

1. A good teacher sets out clear and reasonable goals and expectations.

A good teacher has a crystal-clear vision of sensible goals for the level and subject being taught, taking into account the needs of individual students. A good teacher has reasonable expectations. Some kids put tremendous effort into their work and yet their very best work is judged mediocre by the teacher's standards; a teacher can't ask for more than their best. If the teacher's standards are far too high they can discourage a great number of students along the way. Daily expectations should be realistic, significant to the students, and help them to strive for their best. Those expectations can be a simple routine in elementary school where the teacher insists that each student daily write in her notebook the date, the unit name, and the question number beside its corresponding answer. Even if the child is a terrible handwriter, she and the teacher will know her efforts are fulfilling the teacher's expectations.

How, indeed, does one know what standard or degree of expectation is set by the teacher? One way is through the teacher's comments on tests and assignments. Another is through the interpretation of the reports. When report cards are sent home, they seem to indicate where children stand in each subject, based on a variety of supposedly objective criteria such as quiz and test results, essays, and classroom participation. In addition, the teacher may comment on the student's performance, attitude, and/or behaviour individually and in comparison with his classmates, according to her own expectations. These comments should have meaning to students as well as to parents. If students are confused or unclear about the teacher's expectations, they should ask the teacher to interpret the reports, to explain her written comments on tests and assignments, and to define her expectations so that students and parents know and understand them.

A truly effective teacher explains her expectations to her students. In the higher grades, at the start of each course, she outlines what she anticipates in terms of the students' participation, presentations, term papers, and work. How can you know what the teacher's expectations are? Some teachers send home a contract to be read and signed by both parents and student; a copy is returned to school for placement in the student's file. Check with your child. Some teachers give their students an overview of their general expectations to be kept for reference in their notebooks. Or they will hand out sheets listing project or essay requirements. Often, the teacher will outline to parents at the first school open house or in a newsletter sent home her general intentions for the year. During individual meetings with parents she might explain what her specific goals are regarding the units taught. If parents feel there is no order or meaning to lessons or assignments, if they cannot understand the reason for a certain unit or for homework, they can discuss it at these parent-teacher meetings.

How can you tell if your young child understands what his teacher expects? One way is to check if the child can actually do his work. If he tells you in frustration that he doesn't know what to do with homework or an assignment, then the teacher might not have done a good job of explaining. Or the teacher might have given too much homework and your child can't remember all the steps or details. Students in the lower grades need very careful step-by-step instruction at each stage of a project, as well as examples of what they are expected to do. When assigning papers or presentations, a good teacher might hand out photocopied sheets of paper on which are listed detailed expectations along with the grading scheme.[7]

RECOGNIZING GOOD TEACHING X

A good teacher also helps students set realistic goals. She might identify a situation in which the struggle to pass is causing the student such effort, anguish, and stress that the result comes at a great cost to his emotional health and to his other courses. A good teacher might suggest to such a student that he has reached his limit, that although at the particular time in his life the student may not be not successful in this course, at a later time—even as an adult—he can try again. I struggled with French all through high school, but when I returned to university (as a mother of four young children), French was necessary to graduate. As an adult I had finally learned how to study, and I received As and A-pluses.

2. A good teacher sets various and appropriate levels of challenge.

A good teacher tries to ensure that he stretches and challenges his students' intellects, facilitates their gathering of information, and enhances their learning of skills. In presenting a challenge to the class, a teacher is dealing with a group of individuals, so his demands should be flexible and varied enough that they can be made more difficult for those who can handle more or simplified for those who can't manage the challenge. The teacher circulates about the room, providing individual attention to struggling students on the one hand and, on the other, offering additional material to students who are far ahead of the others.

He establishes a proper level of challenge. He tries to

motivate but is careful not to demand too much, because it might backfire: in her frustration the student might not be able to produce any work, and over a period of time, her self-esteem can be demolished. The opposite can happen, too; if a teacher gives students a task that's too simple, they'll lose interest.

Some teachers are guilty of setting limits on students' abilities by telling them that they shouldn't try something because it might be too hard for them; instead, they should teach them the tools they need in order to succeed. It's amazing how everyone, including kids, will rise to the occasion when it's expected of them. "People of all ages have an astonishing capacity to live up to high expectations. They can also fail miserably if they sense nothing is expected of them," writes Ann Landers.[8]

How can you tell if your child is up to the challenge? Does she ask for your input at every different stage without trying, or knowing how, to do it herself? Does she depend upon you to help her do the entire project? Do you find you are doing it instead of her? Is she avoiding doing her work altogether? Do you find out only at the last moment that she has an uncompleted assignment? Does any of this happen on a regular basis? If the work is too difficult, or if she is not adequately prepared, she might be overwhelmed by the task at hand.

On the other hand, does your child look forward to the challenge? Is she eager to talk about what she is learning along the way? Does she try to do her work independently? At the end, is she proud of her accomplishments?

D. Feedback

1. *The good teacher encourages self-esteem.*

Developing pride within each student should be one of the prime motivations and goals for educators. The significance of a teacher's role in the development of self-worth cannot, and should not, be underestimated. Writer and activist Gloria Steinem believes that self-esteem is necessary for the utmost development of self, whether it be in individuals or in the population of entire countries. In her book *Revolution From Within*, she writes that each person's self-esteem integrates with all those other individuals in family and community to create a nation full of self-esteem. But she also warns that setting expectations too low can adversely affect students' self-esteem and, as a result, their output:

> I thought of all the studies I had been reading on the power of expectation. When teachers of randomly selected students are told their students are slow, they become slower; when teachers believe their students are gifted, they become more gifted...an example of a leader's ability to free the powers of self-esteem.[9]

If students don't feel that they're worthwhile, they're not going to be successful. Although any good teacher wants his students to be realistic about who they are, he also encourages them to work as hard as they can to achieve their potential. With each success they will feel that they are worthwhile people, no matter what.

A teacher who believes in himself, in his career, and in the intrinsic value of self-esteem imparts that belief to his students. To achieve this goal, a good teacher demonstrates respect for each and every student. He values each student's opinions. He gently inspires students to be independent and to take risks. He encourages each student to respond in class with enthusiasm and with absolute lack of fear. Besides teaching them skills, he also encourages his students to observe keenly and to question freely and openly. In other words, skills and confidence go hand in hand; one requires the other in order to be truly successful.

2. The good teacher ensures positive interaction.

The good teacher interacts positively with students. In younger grades, the interaction might be more physical. For example, one marvellous grade two teacher ensures communication with each child as part of her daily routine. At dismissal bell at the end of each day, she squats down to look into the eyes of each of her students, shakes their hands, and says goodbye. Needless to say, her kids adore her.

If you don't have much of an opportunity to see interaction, ask your child if he talks with his teacher.

Does he ask for help? And if so, does he get it? Do *you*, the parent, get feedback from the teacher?

How can you tell if the teacher treats her students well? Older kids will be quick to tell you if a teacher is decent or fair, usually without your asking. But you might have to pump younger ones with questions such as, "Do you like your teacher?" "Why?" or "Why not?" "Is your teacher nice or fun to be with?" "What did you talk about with your teacher today?" or "What did your teacher show you (and your class) or tell you today?"

3. A good teacher guarantees a non-threatening classroom.

A good teacher ensures that students feel safe to learn in her classroom. She guarantees a non-threatening classroom where students can make mistakes. She believes that teaching means never presenting a right and a wrong but, instead, encouraging a process of thinking through and solving problems. Students shouldn't be afraid to produce work lest it be judged either less than adequate or completely wrong. Instead, the teacher uses her students' work to analyze and help develop the skills they need to improve.

A good teacher also allows students the freedom to question. Students should be comfortable to ask anything. People make mistakes if they are too embarrassed or shy to find out the information they need. A good teacher encourages all questions because she needs to be sure the students are following. She is also aware that she learns a great deal about their knowledge by the *kind* of questions they ask. If, for example, a grade ten student asks a question that she thinks a grade three or four student can answer, she knows that the student has a significant gap in that particular area. A good teacher, therefore, tells her classes that no question is stupid. A good teacher will not tolerate students making negative comments about any question. You can ask your child if, when, and how often they ask questions or participate in class discussions. If a teacher tells you that your child is not participating, find out why.

4. A good teacher gives constructive feedback.

Essential to the learning process, a teacher's constructive feedback lets the student know how he is doing and how he can improve. At best, positive feedback reinforces his self-confidence. At worst, it sets the student back on track and underlines new approaches for problem-solving. Feedback is most useful if it is given as soon as possible after a student completes a task, whether it be homework, a presentation, an essay, or an exam.

A valid form of feedback, criticism is necessary to help improve students and their work. The most effective criticism, however is constructive. If a teacher's criticism is too often negative, the child might stop listening or, at worst, lose faith in himself. Aware of the effects of too much criticism, one teacher tries to limit herself to only two criticisms at a time when going over a piece of work with each student. She is careful to point out the positive aspects of students' work, even if the only thing to praise is his effort. Trusting her judgment, students will accept her positive criticism.

A good teacher understands the value of balancing valid criticism with praise. Praise is acknowledgement of an effort made or work well done. It can consist simply of a kind word, a pat on the back, or an encouraging comment on a paper or exam. In early grades, it can be an accumulation of stars or stickers for positive reinforcement; in the upper years, it is best interpreted through both grades and written or oral comments. A good teacher will also teach her students the necessary analytical skills to be self-critical so that they can improve their own work (such as, for example, editing a draft of an essay).

Parents can ask their child if the teacher's critical comments are said in a nice way, and if they help the student to improve. Does the teacher balance criticism with praise? Does the teacher take up work soon after its completion? Does she teach the students how to analyze and criticize their own work?

5. A good teacher is a just grader.

A good teacher understands the importance of grades and grading justly. Grades supposedly represent a definitive indication of where the student stands in relation to his peers and also to his own abilities. Accumulated and averaged out on report cards at the end of each semester, grades also give some kind of evidence to the parents as to how well their children are doing academically. In higher grades, marks can make the difference in being accepted to courses in institutions of higher learning, including universities and colleges. Grades also serve as the major criteria for the awarding of scholarships.

Grades serve as a concrete and easy form of feedback. Grades are beneficial to teachers: delineating the marking scheme in advance can help them to crystallize their aims and objectives for each project. Later, the teacher can analyze the students' grades and determine where she might modify the program to suit individual needs. The teacher can use test marks to tell whether all the students are ready to move on to the next level or unit or whether a few of the students are having difficulty with a particular area. Through the test analysis she can identify what it is that students, individually or as a group, don't know or understand.

A good teacher considers the most effective way to actually mark up the assignments and tests. For example, errors marked with either a big ring around them or a huge mark underneath might emphasize to the student all the errors he has made, reinforcing those errors rather than his accomplishments. It might be more appropriate for teachers to use check marks for work well done and tiny symbols to indicate factual or spelling errors. A good teacher gives marks for work done and not just for the right answer, because the process is as important as the final conclusion. The teacher might indicate also on the answer sheet where or how the student could have improved.

A good teacher's comments, whether written or oral, are always constructive and instructive, indicating where to improve and outlining detailed suggestions. To the student, grades can indicate how much he improved from where he started. Together with the teacher's comments, grades tell students where and why they have done well and—more specifically and most beneficially in the learning process—in which areas they can improve.

Parents can review their child's homework, assignments, and tests to check the teacher's grading and comments. Does the teacher give part marks? Does she recognize work well done? Does she acknowledge a student's efforts to improve? Does she make positive and helpful remarks?

6. A good teacher prepares appropriate tests and quizzes.

A good teacher understands that tests can be valuable to students. Tests give feedback, identifying for students both what they know and what they don't know. Aware that development of study and test-writing skills is of great benefit to the learning process, the good teacher prepares students in advance for the tests. He defines his considerations for grading. He outlines the work to be covered and makes sure that the test covers the unit studied. Some teachers give their students handouts listing the topics that should be studied. A good teacher also allows the students sufficient time to complete the tests.

A good teacher knows that, although students have the knowledge, they might not understand the test or quiz questions and therefore might not be able to answer fully or properly. The teacher ensures that questions are clear, their terminology is familiar, and that they define exactly what he wants in response.

A good teacher analyzes the class test results and, if they are generally poor, considers whether they might indicate that he should review the unit further, perhaps changing his teaching approach. The teacher also considers whether he should entirely overhaul the test format—some students might not be familiar with or be capable of responding to a particular format such as, for example, multiple choice questions He also tries to vary the kinds of tests—oral or written, short fill-in-the-blank quizzes, multiple choice, or longer essay questions—and teaches students the skills required to successfully complete each kind of test.

If your child is having trouble with tests, check whether she understands how to do them. Does the teacher accommodate your child if she can't do one kind of test? Is it a test your child finds useful? Is the test, in fact, testing the student's knowledge, covering facts that have been studied in class? Is it appropriate to the subject?

CHAPTER THREE
The Evidence

Teachers are alone in the classroom with their pupils. It's not easy for us to assess them. We are forced to look at the results, at outside "symptoms."[1]

—Gerald Owen

Unless your child or his teacher tells you outright, how can you know that he is experiencing some kind of problem in school? The best way is to pay attention to your child. Difficulties in school manifest themselves in a variety of ways: some are obvious, others subtle. Any of the following signs might mean trouble.

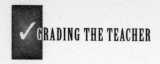

Signs of Trouble

Constant Complaints

Some children with school problems regularly complain about everything and anything in school. They will blame anyone else—but especially their teachers—for their school difficulties or failings. These students might claim that they don't understand what they're expected to do. Some say their work is too hard, or that it's boring. Some will say that their teacher is mean or unfair or simply doesn't care about their problems.

Listen to your child when he complains about school. Question his feelings: "Are you are angry, sad, frustrated?" "Why?" Ask him what exactly is bothering him, and if someone or something in particular set him off. Respect his comments and complaints; they might very well be all too legitimate and point to problems you need to identify.

Skipping Classes

Does your child often start the day saying he's sick? Does he experience stomachaches, headaches, or other physical symptoms? Does he seem to have an inordinate number of injuries during sports activities? Students with school problems will often use any excuse, including a never-ending stream of illnesses and physical injuries, to miss classes. To stay away from school they'll say they don't like the supply teacher replacing their regular teacher, or they need more time

to complete their homework or project. If pressures become too much to bear, some children simply refuse to go to school altogether.

Change in Behaviour

The general attitude or behaviour of students with school problems often changes completely from what you know as the norm, and that change is almost always for the worse. Watch for any unusual fluctuations in behaviour. Has your child become aggressive or troublesome at school and at home? Or is she, instead, suspiciously silent, refusing to talk about school at all? Are you getting complaints from her teacher that she has become the class clown, intent on disrupting the class to draw attention to herself or away from the work she should be finishing? Is she getting into trouble with other children or choosing inappropriate friends? Does she cry easily in frustration about schoolwork or the teacher? Does she wrongly blame herself and need continual reassurance that she is not the cause of her problems? You have cause for concern if the answer to one or more of these questions is yes.

Uncompleted Work

Children experiencing difficulty avoid doing their homework. They say they can't do it, or they need their parents' help. Some of these children frequently leave their notebooks and texts at school. Some "forget" their assignments or their due dates, or leave their work at home so they can't take it up in school. Others say their

work is unimportant, irrelevant to them, and, in their opinion, doesn't need to be done.

Keeping Track

If there is trouble, it might become obvious when you check your child's work. There are three key methods to keeping track of what he is actually learning and accomplishing. The first method is to maintain a constant dialogue; the second is to check his homework and tests; and the third is to ensure ongoing communication with his teacher(s).

Communicate with your child

Not all children are willing or able to communicate what they have learned, but there *are* ways of helping them to share that information with you. Probe. Ask your child what he's been discussing during his classes. Young children might not know that they have learned something. They can't respond to a question that asks "What did you learn today?" And, after a full day at school, older children might not be interested in reviewing their work with you. A question such as "How was your day today?" will usually get an unsatisfying one-word response: "Fine." In my home, I found that rephrasing questions often elicited interesting replies. Try these questions:

—"Did anything interesting happen at school today?"

—"Did you do anything special today?"
—"What's the (funniest), (most exciting), (worst) thing that happened today?"
—"How was the teacher today?"
—"Did your teacher say anything unusual or interesting today?"

Listen when your child is speaking. Train yourself to stop other activities and look the child straight in the eye during conversations. Give the child your fullest attention. You can learn a lot from even the most casual conversation. Many years ago I visited the library with my eldest son, who was in kindergarten at the time. While he browsed through books close by, I became engrossed in a discussion with a friend. After a few moments I realized my son was talking to me and pointing at a picture book that was standing upright on a table.

"What?" I snapped, impatient at the interruption.

"It's a *Tyrannosaurus rex*," he said.

Amazed, I finally sat down with him and asked him to explain what was on the pages. He happily obliged, pointing out and naming more dinosaurs while detailing their peculiarities. I realized only then that his class was studying the extinct creatures. I had no idea until the subject came up that way.

Check homework and tests

A practical method to maintain an eye on the classroom is to check homework assignments. Homework exercises should review knowledge and reinforce it in a meaningful way. Generally based on class work or lessons, homework provides an opportunity to apply newly learned skills. It should represent a challenge to the student, but if it covers too broad an area or if it is too repetitious it can be overwhelming—and it loses its significance.

If your child is having problems understanding or completing her homework, the teacher might not have adequately prepared her for it. Discuss homework as well as projects with your child. Verify that they are completed and corrected. If she does not regularly record her assignments, help her develop a process to do so, or suggest to the teacher that he institute a method by which children keep track of their homework daily.

Another way to monitor your child's progress is to make sure you see his tests. Study them. If the results are not good, analyze why. He might not have studied appropriately or sufficiently. Perhaps his study skills are inadequate and need upgrading. On the other hand, the work might be too difficult or irrelevant.

Test results reveal a great deal about the teacher as well as the student. It is possible that the teacher did not teach the unit well. Or she might not have made it clear what details would be on the test. The test itself might not be well-phrased or suitable for the class. Perhaps the teacher needs to focus more on teaching test-taking skills.

Communicate with the teacher(s)

Regular communication between teachers and parents prevents surprises at report card time; it also allows you to deal with difficulties and problems in a timely fashion. The teacher can inform parents of a child's progress throughout the school year. Many teachers achieve this end by requiring that both parent and student sign not only the term reports but also tests, essays, and projects as they are returned. Parents can also call the teachers regularly to keep apprised of their child's progress, but particularly to notify them of a problem, change of circumstances, or the status of an ongoing situation.

Problems with Children

Any one or more of the trouble signs mentioned earlier in this chapter can indicate that your child is having problems at school. Before assuming that there is a problem with the teacher, check that there isn't a problem with your child. Perhaps, for example, the child has an unrecognized perceptual need such as glasses; he might be hearing-impaired and require an aid; he might have an undiagnosed learning disability and should be tested. A school bully, family dynamics, or lack of proper sleep or nutrition might also be causing your child undue stress.

Investigate. It might help you to call the teacher; tell her that you've noticed some problems and solicit her observations and help. You might also ask your child if she's having trouble seeing the board or hearing the teacher from her seat. Have you noticed that she is lethargic or overly cranky at home because she's up too late at night, either watching television or speaking with friends on the phone? Fatigue might very well be affecting her concentration at school, and you might have to enforce bedtime restrictions. If she consistently works through the night on projects to meet deadlines, then you, the teacher, or a tutor might need to teach her organizational skills. If she's having trouble with basic skills such as reading, writing, or understanding and solving simple math problems, she might need extra help to compensate for a learning disability.

Problem Teachers

If you have conscientiously investigated and ruled out the possibility that your child has personal problems, or if you've dealt with those problems and your child continues to have difficulty at school, you may then wonder if the main cause for concern is the teacher. If you have any doubts or apprehensions, look for any one or more of the warning signs.

Notice how the teacher conducts herself in the class, especially in her treatment of students: are they given unfair tests, including work that has not been covered in class? Pay attention to what the teacher says and how he says it: does he make inappropriate verbal or written comments? Is his tone rude or sarcastic? Notice also what the teacher *doesn't* do: be on guard if your child's tests or work remains unmarked, or if his projects and assignments are not returned until months after their due date.

Teachers have the power to influence their students' academic futures positively or negatively. The effects of bad teaching can be not only long-lasting but even fatal to the learning process. Sometimes the impact does not manifest itself for decades. Unfortunately, it is true that some teachers ignore the pleas of their students for help. Sometimes teachers do not meet the students' needs and are unaware of this fact. However, although students are much too often subjected to the peculiarities and the deficiencies of their less-than-perfect teachers, few teachers are as bad as those described on the following pages.

How do you classify "problem teachers"? Through their words and actions, problem teachers create a multitude of anxieties and stresses in their classrooms. These are teachers who, to varying degrees, impede their students' abilities to learn or to be fully successful. The following categories are general groupings of problem teachers.

Abusive Teachers

Abuse can come in many different forms. An abusive teacher might advocate physical punishment: one principal privately advised his newly hired teachers that the best way to discipline poorly behaved students was to sharply yank their hair or to suddenly punch them in the stomach (in private, of course) because neither left marks. Generally, though, teacher's abuses can be much more subtle and equally destructive. Such abuse can happen, for instance, when a teacher ignores students' questions or denigrates students' answers.

The effects of both physical and emotional abuse can be devastating and lifelong. A teacher who belittles or embarrasses a student either in private or in front of others—especially because of an inconsequential misdemeanour—can traumatize that child. In researching this book I heard the story of a student who was commonly berated and insulted by his teacher throughout the year. It was only with great difficulty, and with the support of his parents, that he was able to overcome and to move beyond the insecurities that were, in fact, created by his teacher. Years later, at his younger brother's graduation ceremony, the teacher approached the older brother and asked him in a condescending tone, "And where are *you* today?" The young man looked directly back, smiled, and answered with one word: "Harvard."

Misuse of Power

Some teachers misuse their power in small ways, such as not allowing an obviously distressed child to go to the bathroom during class time. The power play, however, can be more significant, as in the case of a student we'll call Bruce. In elementary and junior high school, Bruce wasn't a very strong academic student. When it came time to choose courses for his first year in high school, the teacher in charge of signing his registration believed that Bruce would never be able to cope with a normal course of study that would ultimately lead to university. So she refused to sign the high school registration card until he agreed to enter a lower level of study that would take him to community college. In essence, Bruce was virtually forced to enrol in a stream that would limit his future. The teacher thought she was doing him a favour; in her estimation he did not have much potential. However, she didn't take into consideration that he might have been a late bloomer, or that his attitude and abilities might change with maturity. Which is exactly what happened. Soon enough, he had to upgrade all his high school courses, a lengthy, time-consuming process that caused him great embarrassment.

Insensitive Teachers

Other bad teachers are insensitive and misinterpret the reasoning or decision-making of their students. Mrs. Danse (not her real name) is an elementary school librarian. She encourages each of the students in the school to participate in a contest. The object of the contest is to design a poster extolling the joys and virtues of reading. After many happy hours of working together on the project, two young boys proudly took their finished artwork up to the teacher. Giving it a cursory glance, she snatched the colourful paper away from their hands. "Is this the best you can do?" she snapped at them. "It's a mess. Go back and try again! Put more effort into it!" She crumpled the fruits of their labour into a small ball and tossed it into the nearby garbage can. The boys were flabbergasted. Later, one cried to his mother, "We worked so hard to make it good. And we painted it like those famous painters do. You know, like the abstract art we saw in the art gallery." Needless to say, neither boy ever attempted another piece of work for Mrs. Danse. And they both avoided the library as much as possible.

Unfortunately the librarian's actions are not uncommon. Too many teachers destroy their students' work. "I can think of nothing that a kid can write on a piece of paper that gives [a teacher] the right to tear it up in front of him," says Richard D. Lavoie in the video workshop *How Difficult Can This Be?* "Yet it happens all the time."[2]

Unfortunately, there are teachers who wield their control thoughtlessly. Careless individuals can commit a thousand little acts of insensitivity. One such teacher will ask a self-conscious poor reader to read aloud in class. Another, knowingly or not, encourages students to laugh at their classmates who are timid or who give wrong answers. Yet another teacher humiliates children by revealing to the class the students' personal histories, such as a hospitalization, illness, particular hardships, or other issues that arose in private conversations with the teacher.

There are teachers who never mark any of their students' work or tests; they are corrected instead by other students. One teacher I know then obliges the kids to read out to the whole class all the grades so that he can enter them into his ledger. Any student who does poorly on the test is humiliated at least three times. In the first instance, he is devastated that a peer marks the test. (One young adult says she remembers purposely sitting next to a boy who was not part of her circle of friends because she knew he wouldn't care to spread word of her failures.) The second humiliation is the fact of the low mark. The worst degradation, though, is that all the other classmates hear—and react to—the results at the same time as the student.

Dishonest Teachers

There are dishonest teachers who are skilled at concealing their defects from their colleagues and parents. Although they expose their weaknesses to their classes (impossible to hide over an extended period of time), they hide their own deficiencies or destructive attitudes behind a different mask for parents and administrators. They might be razzle-dazzlers, but it's all smoke and mirrors.

Sometimes dishonest teachers are teaching subjects in which they have little or no knowledge, understanding, or experience, and they don't know how to or won't prepare themselves. One high school law teacher uses the textbook verbatim. He sidesteps any questions about the principles of law or their application because he doesn't understand them. Tests are taken from the teachers' handbooks. He grades only the parts of the answers he recognizes from the answer sheets. He gives grades only for answers that are memorized from the original; he won't—because he can't—give recognition to original and logical thinking.

There are dishonest teachers, as well, who might be knowledgeable about the subject but don't know *how* to teach it, and don't attempt to learn how. An example is the art instructor whose lessons have no value or substance. He finds it much easier to make his points by demonstrating right on students' work rather than actually explaining the techniques. This kind of "educator" might appear to conduct interesting programs; in his case, the artwork lining the walls of the school is incredibly beautiful. Yet the students, still mystified, end up with grades for the completed project that, in fact, reflect the teacher's own proficiency and skills. This teacher is suffocating his students by doing their work for them rather than teaching the skills and then providing them with opportunities to practise and develop expertise. Substance and style of delivery are equally important to the teaching and learning process.

Lazy Teachers

There are teachers who are lazy. Without fear of retribution, they take advantage of their positions of seniority to put out the least effort possible. They assign projects or homework that they never take up in class. They use the same tests and assignments year after year. They teach just enough to passably cover the curriculum, if at all. Recently, an excellent teacher told me that her role is to teach to the whole student rather than just delivering information. That kind of dry information,

she said, can be learned in any library, without need of a teacher. The real job of a teacher is to stimulate the desire to learn and then provide students with the proper tools. The lazy teacher doesn't do that.

I discussed this book with a young student who insisted I include a section about teachers whose programs and lectures are absolutely boring. She wondered what could be done to spice up the classes so that students wouldn't have to struggle to stay awake. I suggested that those instructors whose voices droned on without inflection or respite be required to take drama or stand-up comedy lessons to liven them up. But in truth, there is no excuse for any subject or teacher to be boring. It is up to the teacher to discover ways to make the topic exciting and to convey that excitement to the students. Rather than just lecturing at the front of the class, he can vary the program and method of presenting it. He might get the students involved individually and in groups through projects and discussions. For variety, he might use aids, such as slides, books and magazines, posters, overhead projections, movies, and videos. To spice up the unit being studied, he, or his students, might bring guest speakers into class. The possibilities are endless.

Know-It-All Teachers

Know-it-all teachers make the unfounded presumption that their students are as familiar with the fundamentals of their discipline as they are. Perhaps as students themselves these teachers were able to understand new concepts easily. Since all the concepts are crystal-clear to them, they don't understand when or why students don't understand. They certainly can't comprehend that individuals have different learning styles. These teachers have difficulty relating to their students. If they don't care to learn how to teach to individual students' needs, they cannot effectively communicate the subject's key issues or ideas.

Some of these teachers stand at the front of the class droning data or spouting information that has no relevance whatsoever to the students. The students become lost in the very first class; they eventually drop the course or are forced to learn it on their own, or with the help of their classmates and tutors.

Adding insult to injury, these instructors tend to distract themselves and their students as they insert too much confusing detail, or asides that are unrelated to the subject. Students who don't have the fundamentals well enough under their belts are only baffled by these digressions.

Favourers

"Favourers" fancy certain students to the exclusion of the others. Often it's the bright kids, the high-achievers and self-motivators, who shine in the class and are chosen as "pets." Other teachers favour certain students or groups who become the "in" crowd. These teachers "kibbitz" with their favourite pals, throwing them knowing looks from time to time and making the other students feel left out. These pets can do no wrong; they get the benefit of the doubt in any situation and are awarded marks and favours more liberally than the others. The overt relationship between teachers and their favourites undermines the self-esteem of the other students, because they *know* they are being excluded.

Good teachers do not cater to any group without regard to the needs of, and the effect on, the rest of the students. As well, they do not demonstrate or allow in their classrooms any prejudices such as sexism, racism, homophobia, or class consciousness. If they encounter such attitudes among the students, good teachers ensure that the matter is addressed openly, that sanctions for inappropriate behaviour are clearly set out, and that consequences are discussed and followed through.

Stiflers

Some teachers are "stiflers." They don't allow academic freedom in their classes and won't tolerate anyone else's opinions or point of view. In extreme cases, stiflers won't even allow students to ask questions. When confronted by a non-accepting instructor, students, especially those who are already insecure or inhibited, learn to be quiet and not to participate in class at all.

Ann Druyan is a writer and activist who was elected secretary of the Federation of American Scientists. She and her scientist husband, Carl Sagan, have collaborated on myriad projects, including several books and the television series "Cosmos." Druyan was "derailed" from her interest in science and mathematics when a junior high school teacher ridiculed her excitement over the universality of pi, the ratio of the circumference of a circle to its diameter:

> I raised my hand and said, "You mean this applies to every circle in the universe?" and the teacher told me not to ask stupid questions. And there I was having this religious experience, and she made me feel like such a fool. I was completely flummoxed from then on until after college.[3]

In fact, Druyan eventually dropped out of university and began to educate herself.

Saboteurs

Taking personal pride in making their classes as difficult as possible for their students, the "saboteurs" might use "tricks" to make tests difficult rather than truly challenging. They seem to sabotage students' efforts purposely by routinely castigating them, nipping in the bud their pupils' pride and potential to be creative.

Some saboteurs are sarcastic. Sarcasm can undercut students' enthusiasm for learning while simultaneously sweeping away their self-esteem. One saboteur might set aside one student in the class to be the butt of all his ridicule. Another might resort to mocking a student's shortcomings or mistakes, rather than dealing with them in an sympathetic fashion. Another kind of saboteur might pounce on students early in the year, denigrating their answers and making them afraid to participate at all. Sometimes the saboteur's own sardonic tone spurs classmates to laugh at other students' questions and answers. "Constant insults are not going to encourage them," maintains Marcelle Feldman, a private tutor and teacher with more than four decades of experience. "On the contrary, it makes them feel worse about themselves." In a proper classroom environment students should feel comfortable about asking any questions or offering opinions.

Blocks

"Blocks" cross all categories of problem teachers. Like impenetrable icebergs, blocks are virtually unreceptive to change. Considering their information, opinions, and teaching approaches the only acceptable ones, they resist any advice. They do not understand distress, nor are they willing to make allowances for relieving it.

A student I'll name Keith exists in an impossible situation at school because of his block of a teacher. Keith, who is learning disabled, has a hard time spelling words correctly. Since he wants very much to do well, he spends hours practising the words for each week's spelling list, without taking a break or going out with friends. Each week his teacher undermines his exhaustive efforts by dictating whole sentences using many words that the class was not instructed to study. Although all the words he *did* study are perfectly spelled, she fails him, marking glaring circles around his errors, none of which are the words on the list.

When the situation is pointed out to her, the teacher absolutely refuses to change her method of dictation or to accommodate Keith in any way whatsoever.

Some blocks are blusterers, teachers who are puffed up with their own self-importance. Many of these problem teachers are unresponsive, either innocently or wilfully. They seem to ignore their students' pleas for help. Students often feel that these teachers have their own agendas and, as a result, are not meeting the students' needs. Not taking into account the ramifications of their decision-making, these individuals are as irresponsible as those who purposely misuse their power.

Even when they are knowledgeable, indeed brilliant in their field, blocks are totally ignorant, or don't care, about what the term "teacher" really implies. I believe that some blocks actually have their own learning disabilities. Incapable of understanding students' collective or individual essential requirements for learning, this class of teacher either ignores, avoids, or dismisses those needs altogether. I suspect in some cases blocks might even be intimidated by students who don't understand, because they don't really know, or want to know, how to teach effectively.

Shortchangers

Some teachers can shortchange students' potential. A high school counsellor cautioned new immigrant Eva that she'd never amount to much and would never make it through high school, so she should plan her future accordingly. But the young woman believed, and resolved to prove, that she was capable of achieving any goal she set for herself: she eventually succeeded in obtaining her Ph.D. in psychology. "What we ought to be interested in is whether or not students are fulfilling their own potential, what their interests are, and what deficiencies need to be corrected," says Wess Roberts in *Straight A's Never Made Anybody Rich*.[4] Educators can be wrong in their estimation and decision-making; thus they may establish unsuitable pathways or goals for the students, or set their long-term expectations for the students too low.

In *There's a Boy in Here*, a spellbinding account of her experience of raising an autistic son, Judy Barron, lyricist and former teacher herself, sums up her frustrating experiences with experts:

> Yes, experts in the field set limits…I often think of the phrase "self-fulfilling prophecy" which we are warned about as teachers: "If you expect a student to be slow because of IQ-test results and past performance, then the student will never leave the slow track— the child will fulfil your expectations."[5]

If you recognize that your child is capable of more than what the teacher or counsellors say, let them know. Determine to work with the staff, and with your child, to set the right goals for him so that he can decide upon and achieve his potential.

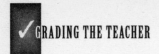

Teachers with No Control

Although being a disciplinarian is only one small aspect of a teacher's role, it is a significant one. Instructors who cannot control their classes, for whatever reasons, cannot teach properly. Therefore, if there are constant discipline problems, their cause should be explored. A good teacher who honours and respects his students above all else is ahead of the game in any kind of situation. A good teacher can work through most discipline problems with her students. In private conversations with them she can often find out if there are specific reasons for the disturbance. Parents can wonder when the class is unruly whether the teacher has not set ground rules for acceptable classroom behaviour.

Poor Communicators

The ability to communicate effectively in class is obviously an essential ingredient of a successful teacher. Unfortunately, the reason some teachers are problems for their students is that they are poor communicators. Some just have a poor command of the language, but others are quite inarticulate. Facility in relating information is a vital component of communication between instructor and students. If a teacher cannot communicate effectively, all the students lose. Students become bored or frustrated in class because they are not learning or understanding information or skills and how to apply them. An example is the scenario of the brilliant physicist who is absolutely incapable of speaking in a language that her students can understand.

Therefore, unless they teach the concepts to themselves, their students are incapable of learning; the base to build the knowledge on is simply not in place.

Good teachers do not just stand at front of the class, talking until the period ends, hoping that everybody in the class understands and gets the concept. If your child is having a problem with a subject, it may be that the teacher doesn't have good communication skills and can't clearly convey the concepts she is teaching. My husband, Paul, believes that the reason why so many people have trouble learning mathematics is because, although many math teachers understand math and "get" it, as a group they can't communicate it—and worst of all, the teachers don't understand why others don't "get" it too.

Few teachers are so bad that they can be referred to as "problem teachers," nor do many exemplify all the utopian ideals described within the previous chapter. Some teachers are better, others are worse, but the majority are, like most humans, fine overall, with some imperfections. Many teachers try to do everything they possibly can to help their students, in spite of the fact that sometimes they will not be successful.

Although as a parent you must be able to communicate with all teachers, it is important to identify those who are posing a problem, and to learn how to deal with them productively in order to get positive results for your child. The evaluation outlined in the following chapter will help you to assess the quality of your child's teacher.

CHAPTER FOUR

Evaluating the Teacher

I wish kids had a report card on teachers.
—Grade six student

W hen I taught in the public school system nearly thirty years ago, a controversy raged over the issue of evaluating teachers' performances and results. No one could settle the questions of who would do the evaluating—peers and/or administrators—what the criteria for valid evaluation would be, what might be the purpose and ultimate advantage of the evaluation, and if there would be demerits or rewards resulting in career or salary changes. After considerable debate, no consensus could be reached, and for a while the issue disappeared, unresolved. As far as I know at no time was the possibility of student and/or parent involvement seriously considered. Certainly, the issues of competence (or lack thereof) and, particularly, accountability were never resolved either.

Teachers were vigorously opposed to the evaluations for many reasons, including anxiety about the fairness of the reviews. They worried that the administration's assessments were not always accurate. Teachers also had apprehensions that the "Old School" (bureaucrats and administrators most likely guided in their careers by self-serving mentors occupying superior posts) would favour its own, a worry that is still felt today. "There is no area of public life other than the military in which positions of policy making and regulatory authority are so totally dominated by professionals from the field," say Jennifer Lewington and Graham Orpwood in their book *Overdue Assignment, Taking Responsibility for Canada's Schools.*[1] Teachers feared then, as they do now, that "mavericks" were just not welcome. They worried that administrators and bureaucrats, preferring not to upset the applecart for themselves, would repeat the cycle by supporting people who shared their values and approaches to education.

Assessment reports on teachers can be as enlightening as students' report cards. Evaluation reports offer valuable feedback to administration. They can highlight good teachers and indicate those suitable for promotion. They can help focus on the major areas of concern, pointing out each teacher's general and specific weaknesses and strengths. Steps can then be taken to reward accomplishments and/or address problems.

Today, virtually all school boards have some kind of process in place for measuring teachers' capabilities and effectiveness. So do individual schools. Generally, in elementary or small private schools, where a small staff of ten means an easygoing exchange among teachers and administrators, teacher assessments are done by school principals. In larger institutions, the task might fall to vice-principals or department heads. In certain circumstances, public school teachers are also scrutinized by board superintendents. Where the situation involves a larger staff and student body and several levels of administration, teacher assessment can be more difficult. The procedure becomes formalized and class visits by administrators are obvious and intrusive.

If parents have concerns about the quality of a teacher, or if there is an unresolved student-teacher problem, they can speak with the school board and administration. Parents have a right to ask if and how teachers are evaluated. They have a right to understand the process of that evaluation, its purpose, and how the information is used. For the most part, they can get that information from administration. Parents should not expect that either the board or school administration will reveal the results of its own individual teacher evaluation reports. This is confidential information, as it should be. Parents can, however, request that a complaint be recorded in the teacher's file. They can also ask that the teacher's records or evaluation be checked for related complaints by others.

Identifying problems and effecting change are two separate issues. "Old-school" hierarchical systems and procedures are sometimes too established and fixed to welcome change. And while most administrators will stand firmly behind their staff—as they should—some will deny the existence of any problem and refuse to address it. Indeed, some administrators are reluctant to follow up on a complaint because they don't have the heart for it, or because they have a close friendship with the staff members in question. Pushing for change can take a fair bit of persistence.

Gathering General Information

In order to evaluate a teacher, parents should be as fully informed as possible. They can accumulate the information they need by investigation: the teacher's background education, interests, and experience (number of years, schools, and grades taught, interaction and results with former pupils); and the curriculum, whether it is appropriate and challenging. To prepare themselves, parents will need to do some research: personal observation, as well as discussions with the specific teacher, administrators, other teaching staff, their child's classmates, and their parents are sources that might be helpful in compiling general and background information.

1. Administration

Principals, or their counterparts, collect their own data on teachers through various means. They can easily see how the teachers relate to people, especially their colleagues. They know whether they arrive promptly, what their attendance is like, and if they get their marks in on time. It is much harder, however, to appraise the quality of the teaching. Most principals run their schools by a method that has been referred to as "Supervision by Walking Around," which means that they spend a lot of time just being in and out of classrooms. That gives them an overall impression of what each teacher's classroom performance is like on a day-to-day basis.

But administrators are human too and they can err in their judgments. It is possible, for instance, for a principal to make rash assumptions. Every year, one junior high school principal confesses, he would identify in his mind the best and worst teachers in the school. But invariably, before the year was out, a parent would demand to have a child moved out of the "best teacher's" class because he or she thought the teacher "stunk." On the other hand, somebody else would inevitably thank the "worst teacher" in the school, saying, "You changed my life." It never ceased to amaze him.

The value and results of superintendents' visits can sometimes be questionable also; the superintendent's evaluation may not be very accurate. A superintendent sits in on one class and observes what is most likely the teacher's optimum performance, since in most cases the teacher has been forewarned of the visit. On the other hand, a nervous teacher might find his performance affected to such a degree that it falls far below par. The visit itself can be little more than a sham, with no effective follow-up, its purpose, perhaps, to mollify complaining parents.

In gathering information about the teacher, parents can turn to principals for general information. If, for example, parents have questions about her background or the curriculum that the teacher won't answer—or if they are not satisfied with her responses—they can discuss general questions with the principal. About her background ask, "Where was she educated? How long has she been teaching? Has she taught at other schools? If so, which ones? Why did she move here? How experienced is she with this subject? What grades has she taught?" There is no harm in asking for information about the curriculum: "Who sets it? What should it cover? How can one tell if it's being taught correctly or if the level is suitable?" The principal should be forthcoming with some information about the teacher that should be useful to your evaluation.

2. Teaching Staff

Parents can speak with other teachers, discussing such issues as what they are doing in their classrooms or their philosophies about teaching. But it is not fair to expect those teachers to discuss the qualities or shortcomings of other teaching staff. Any teacher who would do so would be totally unprofessional. Besides, teaching associates cannot be depended upon to judge their colleagues' performances. Although teachers can sometimes recognize the quality of their peers' teaching abilities and effectiveness, usually their relationship is purely social.

In any case, most staff members are not aware of problem teachers; nor do they know the difficulties students have with teachers, unless students confide in them. An example is the high school English teacher who, near the end of a semester, was taken out for lunch by a group of her graduating students. During the course of their conversation, the students revealed appalling classroom incidents that they and their class-mates had experienced at the hands of several of her colleagues. I asked her if she'd had any inkling of this unacceptable behaviour or attitudes in her ongoing relationships and discussions with these teachers. "Absolutely not," she swore. And yet she did not report her findings to administration: she didn't want to break the trust of the students or put her own job at risk. In similar situations, most teachers would choose not to interfere.

3. Classmates and their Parents

Parents can speak with their child's classroom friends and their parents. They can ask if their school experiences are similar. If not, why not? Is there a common problem? What is it? Can they look towards solutions together?

Parents of high school students might explore the possibility of instituting teacher evaluations, similar to the evaluation sheets used by many colleges and universities.

In post-graduate institutions, the instructor is generally warned in advance of the visit to the class of a representative from that teacher's faculty. Usually the teacher leaves the room while evaluation sheets are completed by each student and then collected. The evaluations are done anonymously for two reasons: first, in order that grades and comments are absolutely honest, without fear of the teacher's retribution; second, to avoid repercussions on individual students. The results of the survey are later tabulated and the outcome is calculated, noted, and acted upon; often the results are considered when the instructor is eligible for tenure. In high school, these forms can be created by representatives of the teaching staff, administration, and parents and completed by all the students.

Another useful evaluation tool instituted at colleges and universities and adaptable for high school students and their parents is a publication that rates the effectiveness of each teacher on the staff, according to various criteria similar to those mentioned in this book's "report card." The data for the publication is collected from surveys completed by students and parents. The results are tabulated and published in an annually revised edition, openly available in the library. Students can use it to choose their teachers and courses.

Parents can approach the principal with these two evaluation possibilities, but they should expect resistance. They might also raise the issue at a parent-teacher meeting.

Utilizing the Report

If there is no universal system of appraisal, and if the school does not support teacher evaluation by parents, then parents can use the report card at the end of this chapter. If weaknesses and certain failures in teachers are not accurately acknowledged within the schools, then we need to develop the resources to identify and point them out. Although not necessarily better than administrators at assessing teachers, parents can bring a different perspective to evaluations.

A report card or evaluation sheet can serve only as a guideline, a jumping-off point from which these weaknesses can be identified. It is my hope that with the proper "tools"—what to look for and how to recognize it, how to gather information and how to assess it—parents can use each visit, conversation, and meeting with school personnel to uncover more information. It is my hope that parents can prepare themselves so that with this cumulative data they can do something constructive—whether it is knowing how to talk or what to say to the teacher, principal, or child, or whether it is the cornerstone of a process that will eventually bring about significant change in the system.

Although parents might want to take the report card into the class and complete it during a classroom observation time—this action would certainly make a statement to the teacher—I must warn them that teachers would consider the very act threatening and aggressive, and rightly so. In addition, one or two visits are definitely not enough to make qualified conclusions, just as they aren't for the visiting superintendent mentioned earlier. It is much better that parents become thoroughly familiar with the issues in the report card before classroom visits, and that they complete it over the course of time with careful consideration.

The best assessments are made by exploring a combination of resources. One important resource for parents' evaluation is their children. Another is the child's homework and assignments. A third resource is presented during classroom observations. And, finally, the fourth comes through meeting and speaking with the teacher.

1. The Student

Parents mustn't underestimate the influence and importance of students as a resource. In fact, their comments at school can help principals get a sense of what individual teachers are like. One principal tells me that kids often bring negative and positive stories to the office. From these the principal builds up a picture of the teacher's actions in class. So, if several students complain about the same teacher, the principal can then take steps to deal with the situation. The stories can work to a teacher's advantage, too. A principal might not think much of a teacher or his methods, but because of what kids (and parents) think and say, he has to conclude that he is a superb teacher—especially if students come back in later years to rave about their experience in that teacher's class.

Parents can, and should, ask for their children's input. The child sees that the parent cares, and the process itself serves to empower the student. If there is a problem, the student will feel that his input helps him and his parents strive towards a common goal. That goal is to improve the calibre of his education, thus enabling him to become more successful academically. The evaluation process can, in fact, crystallize issues that allow for a reasonable and honest dialogue between students, parents, and teachers.

Students are often the best judges of their teachers because, since they are in constant contact, they can't be fooled. Who knows better than the students what is really going on in the classroom, how efficient and effective the teachers are? Some educators have argued that students' assessments tend to be unreliable. Too often, these critics say, students rate their teachers on personality and how they grade papers and tests. But Harry Murray, a professor of psychology at the University of Western Ontario and one of North America's top authorities on student appraisals, reports that those appraisals are "surprisingly reliable and valid." Trained observers, he says, usually come to the same conclusions as the students.[2]

Children of any age can be helpful to the parent's evaluation. Junior high and high school students might actually sit down and help their parents rate their teachers. And both older and younger children can help the parents by answering their questions. For example, if parents want to know about the teacher's fairness they can ask if the teacher treats all students equally well, and if he's flexible in special circumstances. If they want to know about the teacher's availability, they can ask, "Is the teacher available to give you extra help?" To find out about her expectations, they can ask, "Did she tell you the rules at the very beginning of the year so that you know exactly what to expect and what she wants from you?" and "Does she tell you at the beginning of each lesson what it's about?" or "Does she explain clearly what she wants you do each time she assigns homework and projects?"

How organized is the teacher? One way to find out is to ask the child if she prepares the students for tests. Is the teacher fair? Does she provide sufficient time not only to complete tests but to check them over? Is she reliable? Ask if she keeps promises. Does she immediately take up homework assignments? Is the teacher responsive, listening carefully to students' questions, answers, and suggestions? Does she react positively and promptly if and when the student asks for clarification and help? In fact, does the student feel comfortable to ask? If not, find out why. If the student says he is having problems understanding what the teacher wants, parents might ask if the teacher explains the lesson in different ways until the child comprehends. Parents and their children might also discuss situations relevant to them as outlined in Chapters Two and Three.

2. Homework and Assignments

Homework and assignments reveal a great deal about the

teacher's attitude and abilities. If, for example, your child has difficulty with her homework, perhaps the teacher is not communicating well; his instructions might not be clear and concise. Ask the child if she understands the assignments. Can she follow the teacher's directions? If the student is experiencing problems with tests, ask her if the teacher gives ample advance warning of each test. Does he prepare students by, for instance, supplying them with an outline of the exact material to be covered? If she studies all the material, but still has problems with tests, ask if she understands the test questions or format. Check them out yourself. Are they well written?

Returned tests disclose plenty about the teacher's goodwill and the kind of feedback he gives. Does he promptly return all projects, essays, and tests? Does he, not other students, mark the papers? Does he give marks for work done and not just the final answer? Does he write encouraging remarks on the papers? Does he take time to comment privately and make suggestions for improvement on the student's essays, projects, and classroom presentations?

3. Classroom Observation

Classroom observation is another way to get information. Before visiting the classroom, it might be a good idea to familiarize yourself with the curriculum, with information from either the school administration or from the board. In elementary school the teacher has exclusive use of the classroom, and her creativity and organizational skills will be obvious in the way the room is decorated. While visiting the class, parents can check the physical layout. Is it divided into work areas? Ask the teacher why she chose to do so. They can note whether the room is appealing, and if it is originally decorated. Any children's work displayed will tell about the topics covered during the term, the quality of class-mates' work, and the expectations of the teacher. Unlike those in primary school, junior high and high school rooms are often shared by more than one teacher, so the chances for attractive or thematic presentations there are slimmer.

Classroom observations can also include sitting in on actual teaching sessions. At this time parents can direct their attention to specific areas covered in the report card. They can look for the different aspects of the teacher's attitude: her enthusiasm, patience, and sense of humour. By watching, they can eventually appraise her skills, expectations, and feedback. They can study her lesson structure, ability to communicate, and rapport with the students. They can focus on such details as her organizational qualities, which are evident in her preparedness for the lesson, the clarity of her instructions, the arrangement of the room, and assignment of homework. With prior knowledge of the curriculum, parents can look for clues that will help assess the suitability of the teacher's course of study and lesson plans. Are the children interested in what is being taught? Are they bored, or excited to learn? Are they working well on their own? Can they do the work? Do they seem to understand the issues?

Are they participating in discussions?

How do parents get into the class to view the teacher and her interaction with students? The ideal way is to volunteer on a regular basis. When I taught kindergarten there were at least thirty children in each of the morning and afternoon classes. To make the teaching manageable for me and productive for each of the children, I depended upon a handful of parent volunteers to help me on a regular weekly basis. However, if a regular visiting routine is not feasible, then parents might ask permission to sit in on the class. Often a primary teacher will invite parents to attend at appointed times which are then followed up with an interview about their child. Parents can also volunteer to help on field trips or visit the school for a special occasion such as Open House or Music or Drama Nights.

4. Meeting and Speaking with the Teacher

In meetings, parents can note how the teacher reacts. Does he respond promptly when parents call to discuss a problem or set up an interview? Is he receptive to their concerns or suggestions? Is he welcoming? Does he answer questions honestly and openly? Does he seem to be truly concerned about the child? Does the teacher keep in touch with parents about difficulties or problems their child might be having? Does he indicate a willingness to work towards implementing solutions to the problems parents raise? Does he follow up quickly and as thoroughly as he says he will?

Completing the Report

Whatever way you go about it, before marking anything down, reread Chapter Two, which corresponds to
the four sections of the report card. Consider what
components influence your decisions for grading. Are
you being objective and fair?

After completing the report, analyze the results section by section and as a whole. What are the teacher's
areas of strength? Where are the areas of weakness? How
is your child affected? What suggestions can you make
for changes? What kind of assistance do you want from
the teacher? Using the report as a guideline, refer to its
information and results in correspondence and meetings
with the teacher or with the administration.

To simplify grading, I have created only three
response categories:

$$Never = 0$$
$$Sometimes = 1$$
$$Always = 2$$

To tabulate the marks, add the totals in each unit, then
add together the grades of all the units.

Your Child's Teacher:

TERM

REPORT

CARD

Use the following report card to evaluate each teacher. You may substitute your own categories as you will. The marking scheme is as follows:

Never = 0
Sometimes = 1
Always = 2

- Assign a grade to each question accordingly;
- Subtotal the grades for each section;
- Add together all the subtotals;
- The total grades add up to 50.

A. ATTITUDE:

1. ☐ **LOVES TEACHING**
   /2 Is she passionate about her work?
   Does she enjoy her students?
   Is she genuinely concerned about students?

2. ☐ **EXHIBITS GOODWILL**
   /2 Does he want the students to succeed?
   Is he generous with his time and knowledge?
   Is he easily accessible to students and parents?

3. ☐ **RECEPTIVE**
   /2 Is she sensitive to problems?
   Does she respond quickly to requests for help?
   Is she responsive to suggestions?

4. ☐ **SUPPORTIVE LISTENER**
   /2 Does he welcome students' visits and discussions?
   Is he non-judgmental?
   Does he give full attention to students and parents?

5. ☐ /2 **PATIENT**
Does she acknowledge and
account for students'
differences?
Does she patiently accommodate the differences?
Does she take the time to
listen and respond?

6. ☐ /2 **SELF-ANALYTICAL**
Does he offer solutions to
problems in class?
Does he welcome suggestions
for improvement?
Does he change programs or
methods of teaching when
necessary?

7. ☐ /2 **MOTIVATES WITH ENTHUSIASM**
Is your child caught up by the
teacher's enthusiasm and
love of teaching?
Is your child eager to go to
school and to learn?
Does your child enjoy his
homework and assignments?

8. ☐ /2 **HONEST AND RELIABLE**
Is the teacher honest?
Does she honour her deadlines
   and appointments?
Does she honour her word?

9. ☐ /2 **DISCREET**
Does the teacher keep
   confidences?
Does he never divulge secrets
   about others?
Is he reluctant to pry for
   information?

10. ☐ /2 **SENSE OF HUMOUR**
Is the teacher at ease with
   students?
Does she laugh with them?
Does she use gentle humour
   to defuse class tensions?

A. SUB-TOTAL: _____ /20

X

B. SKILLS:

1. [ ] */2* **COMMUNICATES WELL**
Does he have good use of the
language?
Is he able to break down
complicated information
into understandable
segments?
Are his answers adequate?

2. [ ] */2* **KNOWLEDGEABLE**
Is the teacher thoroughly
familiar with her subject?
Is she able to explain the
fundamentals?
Does she indicate she has a
wide-range of interests?

3. [ ] */2* **TEACHES RELEVANT
INFORMATION**
Does he put his subject into
context for the student?
Does he make subjects
relevant to the student's
world?
Is your child demonstrating
interest in new subjects?

4. ☐ /2 **TEACHES STUDY, ESSAY-WRITING, AND TEST-TAKING SKILLS**

Does the teacher teach learning and study skills?

Does she teach essay-writing techniques?

Does she prepare students with test-writing strategies?

5. ☐ /2 **WELL ORGANIZED**

Is the teacher prepared for his lessons?

Does he teach his students how to be organized?

Is he prompt about returning assignments?

6. ☐ /2 **ACCOMMODATES INDIVIDUAL NEEDS**

Does the teacher address your child's needs?

Is the teacher fair?

Is the teacher flexible, making allowances for special circumstances?

7. ☐ /2 **ESTABLISHES AND MAINTAINS DISCIPLINE**
Are the students well-behaved and respectful?
Has the teacher established classroom routines?
Is the teacher fair but consistent in the way she deals with infractions?

B. SUB-TOTAL: _____ /14

C. EXPECTATIONS:

1. ☐ /2 **SETS OUT CLEAR AND REASONABLE GOALS AND EXPECTATIONS**

Does the teacher outline his goals and expectations?
Are expectations realistic?
Do they help students strive for their best?

2. ☐ /2 **SETS VARIOUS AND APPROPRIATE LEVELS OF CHALLENGE**

Is the teacher in touch with the level of work your child is capable of doing?
Do her lessons and assignments adequately challenge the student?
Does he accommodate the student's abilities and previous knowledge?

C. SUB-TOTAL: _____ /4

D. FEEDBACK:

1. ☐ /2 **ENCOURAGES SELF-ESTEEM**
Does the teacher encourage the student to be realistic about himself or herself?
Does he also encourage the student to achieve his or her potential?
Is the teacher respectful of the student?

2. ☐ /2 **ENSURES POSITIVE INTERACTION**
Does the teacher interact positively with the student?
If the student asks for the teacher's help, does he get it?
Do you get feedback from the teacher?

3. ☐ /2 **GUARANTEES A NON-THREATENING CLASSROOM**
Does your child feel comfortable about going to class?
Does the teacher encourage students to answer without fear of making mistakes?
Does the teacher promote the student's active participation in class?

4. ☐ /2   **GIVES CONSTRUCTIVE FEEDBACK**
Does the teacher give
constructive criticism?
Does she praise the student?
Is the teacher's feedback
prompt?

5. ☐ /2   **GIVES DESERVED GRADES**
Does the teacher break down
the marking for the students
and give part marks for work
correctly done?
Is she thoughtful about the
way she grades?
Does she add comments to the
grades?

6. ☐ /2   **PREPARES APPROPRIATE
TESTS AND QUIZZES.**
Does the teacher prepare
students in advance for tests?
Does he allow the students
sufficient time to complete
the tests?
Does he prepare and distribute
different kinds of tests over
the year?

D. SUB-TOTAL: _____ /12

SUB-TOTALS:

A. ATTITUDE

_____   **/20**

B. SKILLS

_____   **/14**

C. EXPECTATIONS

_____   **/4**

D. FEEDBACK

_____   **/12**

TOTAL OVERALL SCORE   /50

SCORING

More than 45 is Truly Outstanding;
Between 40-44 is Excellent;
37-39 is Very Good;
30-36 is Fair;
25-35 is Poor;
Under 24 is Quite Unacceptable.

X

COMMENTS, SUGGESTIONS:

_____

_____

_____

_____

_____

_____

_____

_____

_____

_____

_____

_____

_____

_____

_____

_____

_____

_____

CHAPTER FIVE

Making Changes

Why complain? What's the point? Nothing will change.

—A frustrated parent

I f you have decided that there is a problem with the teaching your child is receiving, it is time to act. It is essential, however, to determine the type of the problem, evaluate its seriousness, and proceed accordingly. There are several possible steps that you can follow. Be prepared at every stage with a clear, rational account of the issue you wish to resolve and with attitudes and strategies that will keep you and the educator focused on the issue.

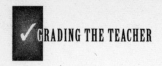

Productive Discourse

When you first contact your child's educator—by letter, on the phone, or in a meeting—be aware of your manner of approach. If you are irate or upset, step back and cool off first. Don't confront anyone when you are very angry; you might shut down the lines of communication before you've even begun. Do not attack, cajole, swear, shout, or lose your temper. Such behaviour doesn't do much for the child, nor does it advance your case. Be composed, collected, and reasonable. You will get much better results if you say calmly, "I'd just like some more information about this," or "I'm not clear on how this was handled."

Evaluate the situation to decide whether it would be beneficial to have your child join you in this or future discussions, particularly if her viewpoint is contrary to that of the teacher. Ask for the teacher's consent in advance before asking the student to attend the meeting. An experienced and confident teacher will probably find such an interview useful; however, an inexperienced or insecure teacher might feel threatened if he believes his word is being weighed against the student's. Sometimes, too, the teacher might feel that there are sensitive issues involved that the teacher should raise without the child present.

Know exactly what issue(s) you want to address; make a list to ensure that all your concerns will be covered. Be open, honest and forthright. Directness is the key. Raise the issue, then ask how it can be remedied in a way that will be mutually beneficial. Pay attention to the response. Consider it. Weigh it. Listen; don't interrupt. Answer questions as best you can.

Assume that the teacher has the student's interests at heart (most do). In any conversations and meetings, ensure that you emphasize your concern for the child's welfare and success, that you intend to help the student, and that you want to enlist the educator's support and input. Any good educator recognizes that parents are acting as advocates for their kids. Therefore, expect him to be sensitive to the fact that you are looking for the best break for your children. Most educators welcome input if they are approached by a parent (or student) who demonstrates goodwill, a clear head, and an even temperament. If you have any positive suggestions, offer them. Welcome advice yourself. Be sensible and realistic in your expectations. Offer to help in whatever way possible, and mean it.

Don't be overwhelmed by "Teacherese." As in any profession, teaching has its own language, idioms, and jargon, some of which is baffling. Parents might try to become familiar with terms in advance (through friends, parents, and other teachers). "If you do some homework and learn some of the relevant dialect, alleged experts won't be able to brush off your opinions," writes Gerald Owen in his article "Ships of Schools."[1] Don't let any educator "beat around the bush," speak in generalities, or cloud his speech with euphemisms. In a polite way, ensure that he or she gets to the point. Don't accept answers that dilute or divert the issue(s). Focus the discussion. Ask for specifics. For example, if you don't know what "working at expected level" means, ask questions along the lines of, "What are the specific criteria expected for that level?" "Who decides on the model?" "Against what and whom is the student being compared?" At no time during your conversations with educators should you be uncomfortable or afraid to ask for explanations of terminology not familiar to you. If you don't understand the answers, or if they are incomplete, ask for further clarification. Persist. Ask until you understand fully. Don't allow any educator to be patronizing or intimidating.

Distinguish also between two types of problems: relatively simple ones that can be quickly resolved; and more complex, wider-reaching ones that need time for resolution. Keep in mind that sometimes what you think is a simple matter might already be or can eventually develop into something more complex. It might require some time and research to find out why. It takes the continuing determination and co-operation of both parents and educators to reach conclusions, establish goals, and map out the steps to achieve them.

I know of one student who was getting into trouble with other kids at school. On investigation, it turned out that his teacher had been picking on him, regularly (and unconsciously), in class. The other classmates, adopting her attitude, took her treatment of him further and began physically attacking him in the schoolyard. When finally hauled to the office, the group blamed him for the fighting. The teacher was soon made aware of the way she'd been treating him and the results of her behaviour. As a result, she was able to work to change her approach.

In another situation—all too common—a student in first year at junior high school played the class clown. Her report card comments from several teachers emphasized that she regularly fooled around in class, disturbing the teachers and other students. Her parents questioned the child and found out that she was overwhelmed by her timetable expectations and workload. In addition, she'd recently been ostracized by lifelong friends. Unable to cope, she was drawing attention to herself in any way she could. Parents and teachers worked together to enhance her self-esteem: first, by helping the child realize that her behaviour attracted negative attention; and second, by teaching her strategies to improve, both academically and socially.

Another student's grades were much lower than his capabilities. Through meetings and discussions, parents and teachers discovered his inability to be organized or to study. Together, they developed a program to help him upgrade those skills. Among other steps, he was trained to record all work in his daybook, and he was privately tutored in some of his weak subject areas. He went from being a C student to one who got As.

A discussion with the educator(s) should clarify misunderstandings or misperceptions on both sides. During these talks, you can verify the details of particular incidents. Once the problem has been identified, try to work out mutually agreeable solutions. Decide who will deal with which issue(s). Finally, don't assume that after your meeting all issues and solutions will be attended to; set a deadline and then communicate again to follow up on progress. Also, recognize that some changes need more time than others, depending upon their complexities. At the very least, set a reasonable deadline to report results. All parties—parents, students, and educators—should try to follow through diligently to resolution.

Approaching the Teacher

If there is a problem at school, you can offer your child the options of 1) handling it on his own, 2) talking to the teacher accompanied by you, or 3) allowing you to deal with the situation. Elementary school students would most likely feel better to have you with them—if they want to be in on the meeting at all. In any case, you can teach your maturing children how to interact and communicate with teachers. With this knowledge, students will be increasingly successful at dealing with school problems on their own. Students from about first or second year junior high school right through high school should have some experience doing so and should be much more able to communicate effectively with their teachers when problems crop up. If your school has designated a staff adviser, he might also be helpful to both you and your child in resolving your problem.

Student Approach

Prior to speaking with the teacher, the older student should focus on the issue or problem that concerns him and try to identify it precisely. If it is relatively minor, then the student might ask the teacher for a private interview. During that meeting, the student can state his case in a positive manner. For example, if the teacher tends to write negative remarks on tests and essays, the student could say, "I would appreciate if you would suggest specific ways to improve," or, "Can you give me exact pointers as to how I can upgrade my marks?"

If, however, the teacher resists, just doesn't understand, is insensitive to a request, or if the student thinks he or his concerns are not taken seriously, he should consider whether it would be helpful, with the teacher's consent, to invite a third person (such as his parent, another trusted teacher, or a guidance counsellor) to join in a meeting with the teacher.

Parent Approach

Your child needs to know that she's supported by you as well as her teachers. Introduce yourself to the teacher at the very beginning of the year. Keeping in touch with the child's teacher signals to him and to the child not only that you care about the child's development but that you will be her advocate. Contact the teacher to give a piece of information, make a suggestion, and especially to offer your appreciation. If the student is reluctant to approach the teacher about a problem or has been unsuccessful in getting his co-operation, then it is time for you to step in. You can communicate with the teacher by making a phone call, sending a note, or arranging an appointment.

You shouldn't wait until a situation reaches a crisis point; it might then be virtually unsolvable. Contact the school to get clarification as soon as you perceive a problem. The first step you might consider is to call the teacher to get his or her version of what happened. In the majority of cases, the first contact is the most useful one. If it's simply an explanation that's needed, and it's given satisfactorily, then the issue might be resolved right then and there. If it's a specific educational concern, or if it's a question of calling the teacher's attention to some simple issue, again, that one conversation with the teacher might be the first—or only—step to solving the problem.

Sometimes, if the problem and its resolution are relatively simple, note-writing might be more immediate than waiting for an exchange of calls and messages. In the letter, state the problem and ask for help with its solution. The teacher might resolve the issue immediately; or she might get in touch with you to advise you of the situation as she perceives it, propose a solution, or suggest a meeting.

If a resolution is mutually agreed and acted upon, then further correspondence is unnecessary. If, however, the problem is more complicated—if you think there might be room for misinterpretation, or if a note or phone call has not produced results—then arrange a face-to-face meeting with the teacher.

At this meeting, enlist the teacher's help by saying something like, "We talked before, but are you aware that my son still doesn't understand fractions? Is there something we could do together to help?" Continue to speak with the teacher whenever and as often as necessary to resolve the problem. However, there may come a point when you decide that dealing with the teacher is not sufficient or that the results of your discussions with the teacher are not satisfactory. If, in your estimation, they are not, then consider your next step.

Staff Adviser Involvement

The second stage in a situation that has not significantly improved might be to call the staff adviser or equivalent at the school, if there is one. At some junior high schools, the home form teacher's role involves more than just taking attendance in the morning: as the staff adviser for each student, he has overall responsibility for recording the students' academic progress; he is also the first line of guidance counselling for all the kids. Many junior highs and high schools have guidance counsellors with whom the parents can meet. One principal suggests that a parent call the staff adviser or counsellor to say something along the lines of: "I know that you're responsible for my son's overall academic program. We're having some problems in mathematics with Teacher X and it doesn't seem to be getting anywhere. Before we go further with this, I think you, as staff adviser, should have the chance to address the issue."

If the problem is still not resolved after that discussion, or if there is no equivalent to the staff adviser at your school (especially in elementary schools), then call the principal. Tell her briefly that you have an issue regarding your child you would like to resolve. Ask for an interview. She will most likely respond by arranging a mutually agreeable time. (Parents should try to realize that principals also have other demands on their time and they might have to adjust their schedules to fit the principal's.)

A Final Resort

If you are so far unsuccessful in your quest for help, if administration refuses to, or just does not, handle the problem well, then you must decide on your next move. Perhaps you can turn to your public school trustee, if you have one. One of the roles of the trustee is to serve as liaison between parents, students, and education administration. Trustees help their boards to set the broad outlines and shapes of what the system is going to do. Some trustees get extremely involved in the day-to-day life of each school in their district. Others trust principals to run the show; they stay quite removed from the schools and get involved only if there's a complaint.

If you don't get results from your trustee, or don't have one, and if your problem warrants the attention and numbers of people involved, you can approach someone at the office of either the director of education or the provincial education ministry.

If meetings with teachers, staff advisers, principals, and trustees haven't resolved the problem(s), you have several choices available to you. Decide which, if any, of these alternatives are possible or suitable for you and your child. You can: 1) hire a tutor; 2) arrange for your child to change classes or teachers; 3) attempt to change the school's procedures for dealing with unresolved problems; or 4) change schools.

1. Hire a Tutor

If the problem is one of skills, a tutor might be a viable solution. Some high schools offer peer tutoring programs in which top students offer their services—as volunteers or for a small fee—to those students who need help in specific subject areas. The arrangement can be short- or long-term. Contact the school office or guidance department for information about this program.

Another option, which can be expensive but might be worth the cost in the long run, is to hire a private tutor. The tutor has the advantage of working one-on-one with students and can see immediately how they are reacting to what's going on: she can note when they're feeling frustrated, when they're enjoying something, and when they're successful. With this knowledge, the tutor can also act as a liaison with her students' teachers, notifying them about her conclusions, working together with them on strategies, and recommending to them suggestions about approaches

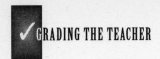

she has found successful.

Your school office, neighbours, classmates, and teachers may be able to recommend private tutors. Notices on bulletin boards of supermarkets, neighbourhood stores, and community centres are another source. Private schools, specializing in tutoring programs, often advertise in local papers, the business section of the telephone book, and on radio. If the tutor is unknown to you and your acquaintances, be wary. Ask for and speak to references. Choose someone who demonstrates some experience in the field. When you discuss the child's problem, request a written or verbal outline of how the tutor expects to help. Ensure that your child likes the individual, because it's difficult for anyone to learn when they don't like or respect a teacher. Decide how often the child will need to see the tutor. After sessions start, keep in regular contact, notifying the tutor about the child's school progress and keeping him up to date concerning any changes or special information about the child that might be useful.

2. Changing school procedure for dealing with unresolved problems

If you feel the school needs a better procedure to resolve problems, you might advocate changes to school (or board) policy or suggest the establishment of a standing committee or council that would represent the interests of parents and students. Appointed or elected, this committee could include persons who are well versed in the workings of the system and who understand the issues. The committee might be comprised of representatives of the school's pupils, parents, trustees, administrators, and teachers.

The purpose of this committee would be multifold. It could deal with unresolved, difficult issues and complaints brought before it by students, parents, and teachers. The members of this council could serve in advisory roles, identifying problems, evaluating them, advocating solutions, and assuring that there is a follow-up. They might also be very useful in mediating in disagreements between parents, students, and educators.

The committee could develop a process to document and monitor complaints. For example, the way the system often works now, a student might complain to the school guidance counsellor about a problem with a teacher. The counsellor denies prior knowledge of any difficulty. She insists that the problem is with the student, not with the teacher. The student knows that other classmates have complained in the past about the same teacher, but the complaints have been made to different staff people. If there is no system in the school whereby these complaints are registered with one specified staff member, then the accumulated effect is never identified or dealt with. A better system for the registration of complaints might include: 1) a central record for cross-reference which could then flag more than one complaint; and 2) a protocol determining the number and severity of the complaints against each teacher should instigate the start of an investigative process.

Another purpose of the council might be to regulate the standard for teaching competency by instituting a students' and/or parents' evaluation of teachers using a report card or form that would be: developed by the school board; created by students, alone or with parents; developed with everyone's input; or based on the one in this book.

The council could formulate a program policy whereby teachers become sensitized to common complaints or problems by parents and students. In this process they might be taught, for example, when and how to upgrade specific skills and change approaches. In addition, the council could encourage teachers to become part of a mentoring program, to undertake counselling sessions, and to take training on tips for conflict-resolution between students as well as between themselves and students.

Try to persuade the administration to adopt your ideas. Or work together with other parents, perhaps through the existing parent-teacher organization.

3. Change Teachers

What if you feel your child is getting poor teaching? What if you feel the teacher is preventing your child from reaching her potential? What if there are serious personality clashes between the two that can't be resolved? What if you feel the student can't function in the classroom as a result of the teacher? What if you think your child is repressed and fearful in the class? What if classroom problems appear too great to be sorted out? What if the student does not have the time to wait for solutions? Depending upon the nature and the gravity of the situation, you and your child will have to decide on a course of action.

For older students, one solution might be to drop the course; if the student needs it, he can take it again at another time in a different venue with a new teacher. Another option is to switch to a new class with a different teacher. Before taking the second option consider carefully if it is feasible to change teachers partway through the year. Indeed, is there another teacher at the school who will appropriately fill in the gap? Will the new class and teacher be better for your child? Might this new teacher's fresh approach and attitude encourage the child's self-esteem? On the other hand, what will the social and psychological ramifications be if the student changes at this point? Will the move end up penalizing the child? Will she lose some of her friends? How will the move effect the timetabling? (In junior high schools and high schools, often changing one teacher means changing all the other teachers as well.) What will friends and acquaintances say or think? Will it matter or have an effect on the student's feelings? If the relationship between your child and his teacher is not working, will it continue to haunt the student even after he moves on to another class at the same school, by influencing the way he is treated or viewed by the new teacher?

In the end, you might decide that moving your child to another class within the school would stigmatize her.

Such was the decision of a family I met who were unhappy with their daughter's enriched program. Her parents felt that she'd lost her self-confidence and that her teachers were not helping her to fulfil her potential; they also felt their honest concerns were being brushed aside. Prepared to move out of her class, the child was nevertheless worried she'd be labelled "a loser" by schoolmates if she left the special program. Therefore, the family settled upon a new school. Welcomed by her classmates and teachers, she quickly adapted to the fresh situation, became a confident leader, and graduated the next year as a valedictorian chosen by her peers and teachers.

4. Change Schools

If changing schools seems the best option, consider first what kind of school you want: public, private, within your area or outside it. It might be difficult to transfer from one public school to another. If you are looking at a school out of your neighbourhood, its enrolment might be filled. Registration regulations often ensure that the school accommodates residents within the district before those living out of district. Switching sometimes requires permission from principals of both outgoing and incoming schools. In addition, some boards require out-of-district students to pay a tuition fee.

Private schools are a second option available to parents who can afford them. Depending upon the province and your ministry of education, you might also have access to charter or alternative schools, which emulate certain advantages of private schools but without their expense. The fourth possibility available for determined and competent individuals is home schooling.

In deciding on a kind of school, consider your child's individual requirements (along with the factors raised in Chapter One). Not every type of school will serve the needs of, or be right for, every student.

PRIVATE SCHOOLS

Parents choose private schools over public institutions for various reasons. Some are disenchanted with what the public system offers. Some have the perception that private schools have less red tape and bureaucracy and, therefore, issues will be dealt with more quickly and efficiently; because they are paying, parents also expect to have more clout. Many parents expect their children to be less distracted, more focused, to have more hands-on experience and personal attention in smaller, private classes, which usually number from a handful to no more than eighteen students. Most parents hope the private school will develop and fulfil the child's full potential. Indeed, a private school education can be more tailored to an individual's needs, and its teachers are usually more available for extra assistance.

On the other hand, parents should consider the several disadvantages of private schools. Tuition is expensive and, for the most part, non-refundable (although a few private schools offer scholarships for a limited number of needy students). Extra costs include textbooks and other school supplies, out-of-school trips, and, in some cases, uniforms (although some parents claim that a regular wardrobe is more expensive). Extra tutoring to bring the student up to class level may very well be an additional expenditure. Another cost factor to consider is boarding for students living far from the school. Distance is a factor for those who must commute, a problem that might be overcome with carpooling or, once again, with an additional cost for hired transportation.

If you are considering moving your child to a private school, research the school and its policies well. Not all private schools have all the facilities available to public schools. Instead they rely upon community resources such as the neighbourhood Y, local libraries, and public parks. Also, while parent participation is generally welcome in volunteering and fund-raising, not all schools invite parents to play a role in policy-making. And even in private schools the quality of teaching is only as good as the individual instructor. There might not be alternatives if the teacher and child do not get along.

ALTERNATIVE SCHOOLS

An alternative school might very well be another route for you or your child to follow. In many ways, alternative schools resemble private schools in that each has a separate identity, an approach that is different from and more specific than traditional schools, small classes, and more flexible and personalized instruction. In Ontario, these schools can run the gamut of educational levels from kindergarten right through to adult, but usually they're divided into primary, junior, intermediate, and senior schools, or any combination thereof.

Alternative schools can be initiated by like-minded parents in the district who share common principles and goals. These parents work as a co-operative, planning programs and hiring teachers, in addition to volunteering extensively within the school. Set up and funded under the public education umbrella, these schools can also be created in response to a need identified and defined by teachers and administrators, as well as boards of education. Those needs are varied and are addressed with specific objectives and specialized programs of study. The school might emphasize parent participation, an arts academic curriculum, students who are highly motivated to work independently, or students who are gifted. One alternative school in Ontario was designed "to preserve and enhance the culture of Canada's Native peoples"[2] and has native and non-native students; the curriculum of another takes its direction from the students themselves; yet a third began as a private bilingual school and has since been incorporated into the public system.

Alternative schools often operate within the confines of an already established, traditional school, sharing its administration and resources. The Ontario high school Interact is such a school. It caters to students who do not fit into regular programming: kids who are training to be professionals in the arts and sports, who can't attend a regular high school because of their schedules and who need an academic program with a very flexible timetable. Existing within the same building that houses the more conventional Vaughan Road Collegiate, Interact is provided with four rooms on the top floor of one wing. Although it shares space, including library and cafeteria, with Vaughan, Interact operates separately. The schools share a principal, although Interact has a program director, who also teaches. Team teaching is encouraged. Two teachers share each room. Classes are small, varying in size from one to fifteen students; if only one student signs up in a subject advertised in the calendar, it will be offered, unlike other schools which require a minimum enrolment. Even an unadvertised subject will be taught to a student needing it for matriculation. Interact offers the core academic subjects but doesn't have the facilities for the rest, such as physical education, art, and music. Its students can study those subjects in the formal program in the regular high school.

Except for the cost, the disadvantages of alternative schools are similar to those of private schools. Not all students thrive in these conditions. For instance, a free-flowing school environment would not suit a student who works best within a highly structured framework. Resources, equipment, facilities, and extra-curricular programs might be scarce or non-existent. The success of the program depends upon the co-operation of parents, students, and teachers; if their philosophies about the school differ or change, its very existence can be threatened. Students might not receive as well-rounded or extensive a program as is offered in the traditional school because small staffs mean that not all teachers can or will teach all subjects, so certain areas like music might be either neglected or left out altogether. (To accommodate this problem, the parents at some alternative schools hire extra staff at their own expense, which they try to cover with monies collected through intensive fund-raising enterprises.) Another drawback to alternative schools is that most students must travel great distances to attend, and they cannot easily socialize with their classmates after school hours.

CHARTER SCHOOLS

Another kind of educational institution currently developing momentum across North America is the charter school. As with alternative schools, charter schools are public schools offering different or enhanced education to improve student learning. Each charter school concept is different from the others because it is developed according to its particular context.

In Canada, the only province with charter schools operating is Alberta. Alberta's ministry of education has been at the forefront of this ground-breaking movement. It has approved five such schools, three of which are in operation now. Charter schools can be created when like-minded parents feel their children would benefit from a particular kind of program not offered in the local school. An application form must be completed and submitted to the ministry outlining the proposed location, the school's charter, how it will be different from the local public schools, how it will operate, the program and methodology proposed, and the kind of results expected. In Alberta, to be educationally and economically viable, the minimum required enrolment for a charter school is seventy-five students.

Charter schools are approved by and established under the auspices of the province's ministry or department of education. Although existing within the jurisdiction of their school boards, charter schools are operated by a corporate entity separate from it. Technically operating as public schools which offer the fundamental basics of reading, writing, math, and science studies, charter schools differ from traditional public schools in key ways. Teaching of all subjects might be based on a particular philosophy, such as the charter school whose subjects are taught according to the methodology used in teaching Suzuki music pupils. There might be a greater depth or breadth of study in subjects such as history or math. One charter school might offer programs for gifted and talented students. Another might be created purely to appeal to street kids or any students at risk. A third might possibly be an all girls' school with an emphasis on women's studies. There is even a charter school in Alberta that caters to the average kids who demonstrate a predisposition for working hard. This school gives its students an opportunity to work independently. As well, it teaches them how to study, how to research, and how to work, whether individually, in pairs, or in groups. In other words, charter schools are innovative and different in that they address certain skills and collective issues in a way that, for whatever reasons, the conventional school does not.

Similar to private schools in that they cater to individual students more than the traditional public schools do, charter schools are different in that they offer public school benefits. For example, charter schools do not charge tuition fees, although parents might be expected to pay extra for materials and resources. Also, if there is room available, charter schools cannot deny access to any student; parents can petition the education minister to review a denial. Furthermore, they can also ask the minister to review extra fees as well as student expulsions. (To find out more about charter schools, turn to the appendix at the back of the book.)

HOME SCHOOLING

According to Wendy Priesnitz, founder of The Canadian Alliance of Home Schoolers, nearly 40,000 children across Canada are being taught at home. Often the decision to home school is made from a religious perspective; many home-schooling parents are Christian and connected to a larger network. Many parents, concerned about their children's socialization, welfare and/or education, home school in an effort to strengthen family values.

Policies about home-schoolers vary from province to province. In the Northwest Territories, for example, although home-schooling parents can set their own curriculum program, their individual boards must approve it. And not all home-schoolers follow guidelines set out by their ministry. Leith White, president of the Alberta Home School Education Association, says his organization would rather that government regulation be minimal. In that province, schools can include home-school students in their registered enrollments, but each school board has been working with home-schoolers in different ways. Wanting consistency, the ministry has been negotiating to establish a basis on which home schooling can operate. Currently, however, only about 30 percent of home-schoolers are registered with any boards, with about 12 percent solidly underground.

To teach at home, the parent must be willing to devote a consistent and enormous amount of time and energy to this significant enterprise. In order to deliver a high-quality, useful program, he must be able to teach all subjects effectively. It would also be beneficial if the parent has the attributes of a good teacher outlined in the early chapters of this book.

Problems will arise if parent and child cannot get along in close quarters over a long period of time. In that case, who will the child turn to for help? As well, there is a danger that children being schooled at home might lose touch with other children, particularly those their age. A parent who chooses this route must allow regular and ample opportunities for the child to socialize. Without entrance exams similar to the American

SATs, there is a concern about home-schooling "graduates" being accepted into universities. To overcome this problem, some home-schooling parents form a loose affiliation with a high school.

I would recommend that any parent in the early stages of decision-making about home-schooling do considerable research, including contacting a home-schooling umbrella organization. To find information about home-schooling, approach your provincial education ministry, local board, and libraries. As well, some retail stores that specialize in educational material sell resources for home-schoolers and might be able to provide you with contacts. (For a list of home-schooling publications, support groups, and individual people to network with in your area, see the appendix.)

Making changes, whatever they may be and to whatever degree, is not an easy enterprise. Although it's not impossible to change the system, it can definitely be a formidable task. "Parents have an absolute right to express their views and make a difference in the school system," says Francesca Piredda in a *Report to Parents*.[3] Don't expect any or all changes to be implemented immediately; it takes time to work through the system. Issues might be more complex and difficult to treat than you imagined. Prevailing attitudes might need time to be modified or transformed. If you have the time to do so, become an active part of the process of change. If you don't, or can't, then look to assorted alternatives.

CHAPTER 6

Understanding the Roles and Responsibilities of Students and Parents

A real thrust in education in the past decade [has been] to bring parents on board, [for parents] not to feel that they send their kids to the "building."

—Linda Miller

A good teacher can be the keystone to a good education, but parents and students themselves are the other essential elements. A student's learning experience and academic success are most definitely strengthened when each group takes on with vigour its own particular obligations.

Students

Parents can help their children understand that students have a vital role to play in their education: learning is a

two-way street. It's not only up to the teacher to teach
effectively but also to the student to make a concerted
effort to learn. Parents can encourage students to take
charge of their education by maximizing the time they
spend learning and the quality of the effort. Parents
can explain to their children that as students they have
at least three significant responsibilities: to accept
responsibility for their actions; to keep parents and
teachers informed; and to demand good teaching.
Parents can describe those responsibilities and take the
students through the necessary steps to play their role.

Accept Responsibility

As a parent, you should make it clear to your child that
you expect him to accept the consequences of his
action—or inaction, as the case may be. Students
should do what they're asked to do to the very best of
their ability, applying themselves to learning and to
schoolwork. Study for tests, complete homework and
other assignments (as instructed and on time), be prepared for each class, and participate to the fullest during discussion period. It's difficult to argue with a
complaining teacher if students simply are not doing
the things they are expected or asked to do. Students
have no one but themselves to blame, and they can't
expect their parents to defend them if they skip classes,
do not attempt or complete assignments, or are sent to
the office for causing trouble in class or on a trip.
Students must be willing to accept the repercussions
for their negative deeds, whether that means failing a

subject or being banned from future trips.

Keep Everyone Informed

Students should be expected to keep everybody—parents and teachers—informed about circumstances and situations that are important for them to know. There may very well be events or situations, school-related or not, that affect students' performances at school, preventing them from completing tasks adequately. For example, students should tell the teacher if they have trouble with multiple choice or essay-type tests, even if they've studied and learned the information thoroughly. They might ask either for more test-writing instruction or for the opportunity to write the test in a different format. Teachers need to know if students haven't been feeling well, if there is illness in the family, or if the parents are breaking up. Most teachers will respond very well to students who experience problems and have previously demonstrated their sincerity, reliability, and determination to do as well as possible.

Demand Good Teaching

Students must also expect, and even demand, quality education. In spite of what many students think, they *can* make a difference. They can teach teachers. They can contribute to the learning process by insisting that they be taught in ways that encourage and allow them to learn.

Students should be encouraged to stop their teachers every time they don't understand something. For example, verbal explanations are not enough for many individuals to learn a concept or method. If they are visual learners, they need a demonstration. There is nothing wrong with a student asking a teacher, "Can you draw a picture or diagram for me?" or, "Can you say it, or show it, in a different way?" Students should feel perfectly comfortable to ask for explanations to help them understand the concepts taught or how to do assigned work. If the student doesn't understand the process, he might ask, "Can you *show* me exactly *how* to do it?" This does not mean the student expects the teacher to give the answer or to do the homework; rather, he is asking for a way to approach the problem. Another way of framing the same request might be, "Can you outline the procedure for me?" or "Can you explain the thinking behind that answer?" Then, to ensure there is no misunderstanding or wrong interpretation, the student might want to verify the information or instructions by repeating them to the teacher. If uncomfortable with interrupting the class or disrupting the lesson, students can approach the teacher afterwards with questions or a request for an appointment.

Parents

Parents are no less important to children's education than are students and teachers. Their responsibilities are: to support the children and the school; in whatever way possible to become involved in the school; to know how much to be involved and when to step back; to support the teachers, giving them positive feedback; and finally, to have realistic expectations.

Support the Children

First and foremost, it is important that as a parent you let your kids know that you love them. Be sensitive to the reasons for their moods, and to their needs. Even after a major fight or disagreement with the child, before the kid gets out of the car or leaves through the door, say something like, "All right, I wasn't happy. You didn't clean your room/make your lunch/do what I asked you to do. I'm upset about that, but I still love you and I want you to have a great day at school and don't worry about it. We'll deal with it when you get home." Too many times an unresolved argument, left hanging in the air, can set the kids off. (Even though they might be teenagers, and parents don't think they care, those kids will have a lousy day.)

Show your child the way to success in schoolwork. Help her get organized. Arrange a proper workspace. Together with her, set up a realistic timetable for working at assignments; ensure it is functional, and that she can keep to it. Look over her notebooks and, if necessary, suggest ways to improve: "The pages might be neater if you use a sharper pencil and erase your mistakes with a clean eraser, rather than scratching out the words"; "It is easier to correct your answers if you number them"; "Take more time to think and then write carefully so that your answers are more complete and legible." Recognize idiosyncrasies in study habits.

One of my sons claims to be able to study with the radio on; I, on the other hand, find it hard to concentrate when surrounded by distracting background noise and movement. Another son can focus only if his hands are busy kneading or playing with a small object. If it truly works, any technique of studying is appropriate for the individual.

If you can, and if they need your help, teach the children study habits and techniques. Show them how to review their material for tests. To help them learn the information, demonstrate how they can break the facts down into small, manageable portions. Give them hints on how to remember facts. Help them to understand and memorize definitions; if possible, connect the meanings to their experiences. Show them how to correlate different pieces of information. Quiz the children orally, or write out little tests. Offer to edit their essays with them, rather than for them. Explain your thinking process when editing so that they will learn. Ask questions that get them to think.

Acknowledge their efforts. Be positive in discussions. If they've improved, let them know you're aware: "You really put in a lot of effort. You must be proud of yourself." If, on the other hand, they are disappointed in a grade, analyze why they did poorly: "This test (essay, project, homework assignment) is not that bad. What troubled you most about it? Let's look at how you might improve next time." Calm their fears. Assure them that you support their endeavours and will be available for them whenever they need you.

Support the School

Educators contend that parents have a responsibility to be advocates for their school as well as for their kids. Studies show that if parents support what the school is doing, then school and student results will be more successful. Some principals get frustrated because they see parents as always wanting things, and not necessarily being willing to help out. Parents should try to assist in the operation of the school in whatever way they can, whether that means helping out when it's needed or being on the parents' advisory committee to develop policy.

Become Involved

Parent involvement is important. There are myriad productive opportunities available, depending on your personal commitments, interests, and time constraints. Find out what is happening at school. If you are able to, visit the school at least once during school hours just to see what's going on. Feel free to communicate with the child's teacher, especially if there's a problem you want to keep tabs on. Discuss what steps you can take to help the child at home or at school.

If you have or can make spare time, join a powerful force: become a volunteer working in the school.[1] Work in the office answering phones, assist the teacher in the classroom, chaperone at least one class trip, volunteer to help during lunchtime, offer to lead an afterschool program, participate in a Careers Day event at the school. Parents are more inclined to be involved in their children's education in the primary to junior grades and tend to withdraw their participation when the students reach high school. Many high school staff and administrators *want*, and try to encourage, parents to stay involved. Get together with like-minded parents. Join or help establish the school's parent-teacher association (PTA).

As a result of continued pressure from well-organized parents' groups, the importance of parental input is becoming more and more recognized at the level of policy-making as well. With a little bit of research you will most likely discover a number of existing parent advocacy groups.

You can become part of your Home and School Association, serving the local community, or you can become associated with provincial or federal groups like the Canadian Home and School and Parent-Teacher Federation (CHSPTF) which has provincial chapter affiliates, a head office, and an executive director. Offering provincial and national seminars and conventions, this century-old organization prints newsletters, reports, guidelines, and pamphlets. Its objectives include keeping members informed about educational trends and emerging issues affecting education, advocating change where it is required, and developing and implementing research projects. It furthermore represents parents on national committees dealing with education, science and technology, the environment, health, and social issues. It also communicates with other national education organizations and the federal government. (To contact the

CHSPTF, see the address given in the appendix.)

Look into the provincial or territorial chapters of various parent advocacy organizations across the country. For example, the Ontario Coalition for Education Reform (CER) is an umbrella organization of parents, teachers, trustees, and ratepayers who seek to improve the province's public primary and secondary schools in several basic ways, in addition to creating an education system accountable in its core curriculum, performance standards, and operational efficiency. One of the seven group members of the Coalition for Education Reform is the Educators' Association for Quality Education, an organization of teachers and other school support personnel dedicated to accountability and effectiveness in Ontario public education. Another member, the Ontario School Board Reform Network (OSBRN) is a coalition of individual reform-minded trustees and concerned taxpayers. The Organization for Quality Education (OQE) is a parents' association with chapters across Canada. For specialized parents' organizations, contact your school board, trustees, or provincial ministry of education offices. These organizations often publish newsletters filled with loads of information on trends and important issues in education, listings of videos, magazines, books, and upcoming conferences. (See the appendix for names and addresses.)

Help implement or participate in a parent council or advisory committee. Led by Quebec in 1972, an increasing number of provincial ministries have been legislating such councils into existence. The Ontario government, for example, has mandated that every school have its own parent council, chaired by a parent, by June 1996. There may be provincial parent councils, as well. The Ontario government recently established an Ontario Parent Council, made up of eighteen members. Six of those members are recommended by regional committees representing teachers, parents, school and school board administrators, trustees, and ministry staff. Three members are recommended by the Ontario Federation of Home and School Associations, the Federation of Catholic Parent-Teacher Associations of Ontario, and the Fédération des associations de parents francophones de l'Ontario. The remaining nine representatives are chosen by the Ministry of Education and Training. The Ontario Parent Council's main role "is to advise the Minister on issues related to elementary and secondary school education and to suggest ways that parents can become more involved in their children's schooling."

The influence and authority of parent councils can be quite significant. Authors Jennifer Lewington and Graham Orpwood propose that parent councils address such issues as "curriculum requirements, reporting to parents, hiring, staffing and promotion, equity and opportunity for all students, school goals, behaviour or discipline codes, homework policy, standardized evaluation, accountability, budget, [and] fundraising."[2] Although many educators are afraid of the potential power of parent groups or councils, Maybelle Durkin, executive director of the Canadian Home and School and Parent-Teacher Federation stresses that they can take a lot of the pressure off teachers. As an example, she says the council can address social problems in the community, where they *should* be dealt with. In addition, parent councils can also deal with values-laden issues that teacher should not necessarily be involved with (such as birth control). Schools can then focus on their primary purpose, which is to develop the children's full potential so that they will function productively in society.

Vote for the best candidate in school board elections. Or, if you have the passion and commitment, run as a candidate yourself. According to Gerald Owen, "these elections are, arguably, more important than national elections."[3] As an elected school board member, you can make a big difference, expressing your viewpoints and working with all the elements in education—bureaucrats, school and board administrators, teachers, students and parents, as well as the community at large—towards implementing your ideas.

Know How Much to be Involved

There are times when parents go overboard with their involvement in their children's school affairs: they fight all the battles and the students don't learn how to speak up for themselves. Instead, encourage your children to be independent, self-sufficient, and to handle their own problems and stressful situations. Allow them to make connections with the teachers and resolve issues on their own. Learn when to start and when to hold back a little bit.

When encouraging your children to ask questions and to tell the teacher when they can't understand, you can guide them with advice and explanations. Through such techniques as play-acting at home, you can prepare even young children in various scenarios, prompting them with leading questions: "Why do you want to speak with the teacher?" "What are you expecting from the teacher?" "What will you say if...?" "If she says or does..., what will your response be?" Give them advice, and teach them strategies to communicate with the teacher. (Reread the section Approaching the Teacher in Chapter Five.) The object is to give the children the skills and the confidence to deal with situations when they arise.

Support the Teacher

Try to be supportive of teachers. Teacher-bashing by parents and the media not only demoralizes the teachers, it also demoralizes the kids and makes it hard for them to be enthusiastic about school. Instead, try to teach your children how to interact with their teachers in a way that is mutually advantageous.

In addition, if you have any information about your child that would be beneficial to teachers, let them know. The most sympathetic teacher can try her best to be in tune with each child, but any one student in a class can hide a lot of things. Teachers in high school point out that they see students for about an hour every day or every other day, and since each child is just one of many, it can be difficult to notice if a student is having problems. If you observe changes in your child's behaviour, or if you have information that is crucial to his well-being, call the teacher, and possibly the administration, about it. Give them the information they need to work with you for the child's benefit.

Accept the fact that your child might require help or guidance outside the school. Negative attitudes, unusual behaviour, or poor school performance might very well be the result of problems that are caused by the teacher, but be open to the fact that there might be other forces affecting your children. Be an advocate for your children, but also be sensitive to special situations and turn to professional counsellors or therapists if your child's needs warrant it.

Feedback to the Teachers

Give positive feedback to the teacher. Offer suggestions for improvement. The teaching staff really needs to feel that they have the support of the people with whom they're working. Don't phone the school only when you have a complaint; call also to say you are pleased, that your child is having a great experience at the school. Write letters or notes expressing your thanks. At the end of the year, tell the principal that your child had a great year, and thank him and the teachers. Or send a letter extolling the virtues of the teacher to administration, with a copy forwarded to the teacher.

Although it is not necessary, you might offer the teacher a token of appreciation, like a nominal gift, a card or note of thanks, or an invitation for tea or lunch. When I taught in elementary school and the parents of one of my students gave me a bottle of homemade wine, I appreciated the gesture so much that I kept it for years, unopened, as a souvenir. You might help instigate an award and presentation ceremony for the best teacher within your school, district, or family of schools. Decide on the criteria for each award, who should vote (staff, students, and/or parents), and a noteworthy prize—perhaps a scholarship in that person's name.

Realistic Expectations

Keep in mind that no situation is absolutely perfect. What is good for one child might not be for another. A teacher with a great reputation might not connect with your child. Or the teacher someone else says was not good for their kid might be great for yours. A fabulous administrator or an excellent teacher can retire, be promoted, or move away. Your school might have an exceptional staff, but your child could get stuck with the only "clunker" of the lot. Sometimes the personalities of student and teacher just don't mesh.

Try to be rational and fair about your expectations of the school system and the individual teachers. Sympathize with the teachers and remember that they have pressures and personal obligations, which, at times, are capped by demanding parents who ask for too much, too soon. Teaching burdens are indeed great: paperwork, school politics, curriculum constraints, and personal demands—to list just a few.

Overwhelmed by escalating administrative tasks, teachers also have to keep up with changes to the curriculum, the challenge of modern technology, and a rapidly expanding information base. (The next chapter deals with those pressures in more detail.)

Have realistic expectations of teachers, especially at the beginning of a year or a new semester. They might be nervous or easily intimidated—particularly those new to the system or the class. They need time and space to develop not only their relationship with students but also a working style of teaching, evolving from the students' needs. It can take a while for both the teacher and the students to develop a rhythm in the class and a sense of security.

Try to to understand the pressures and responsibilities of teachers at the different levels. Elementary school teachers have a lot more discretion with curriculum than do teachers in junior high and high school. They can be more flexible in planning programs within the ten-month period of the school year; they can more or less change units and concepts around at whim or as the need dictates. This flexibility is advantageous to children in the primary grades in that they are more likely to be able to learn at their own rate. If a teacher finds that a particular child just cannot manage a specific concept or activity because he or she is emotionally, physically, or socially not ready to handle it, the instructor can wait even a few months to reintroduce them to the child. In high school, however, the teacher has a set curriculum to follow and very specific time constraints.

He teaches a unit of information, tests the students, and continues until the course is finished, in time for term and final exams. Because of the exams, he has limited time to review difficult concepts or to spend with individual students who have particular problems.

Each age group presents a special challenge to the teacher. Smaller children need more supervision and demand more of their teachers' physical energies. Young teens might be able to work more independently, but their physical and hormonal changes, along with peer pressure and disappointments, create a variety of distinctive obstacles for teachers to confront and overcome. And the attitudes and struggle for adulthood of older high school students present their own significant challenges to teachers, too.

A child's ability to learn depends upon his personal capability and capacity, but his actual success in learning hinges on his inner motivation: he must want to learn. To accomplish that end, he must be prepared to fulfil his obligations to himself, as well as to his teachers. Though the individual teacher's attitude and her methodology can affect the student's motivation, it's often the parents' stance on education in general and support of the child in particular that can be the greatest influence on his results. Indeed, each of the points of the triangle—teachers, students, and parents—are equally important to the learning process. And, if they all work together, the process and its results are immeasurably enhanced.

CHAPTER SEVEN

Understanding Teachers

I am teacher, mother, drill-sergeant, policeman, confessor, psychologist, juggler (schedules/responsibilities), tutor, etc. Everyone expects maximum results with a minimum input—kind of like a mutual fund. People no longer deal well with disappointments/setbacks and tend to give up instead of applying themselves. All the things you listed are valid pressures. Hey! Teachers are only human.

—Anonymous teacher, Calgary, Alberta

Kindergarten students often think their teachers live, breathe, and eat in their classrooms twenty-four hours a day, seven days a week. The children cannot comprehend that their teachers have outside lives with families, friends, and commitments. Indeed, most dedicated teachers frequently feel that their personal lives and families are kept on the back burner, secondary to their demanding careers.

Apprehensive about their careers, often fighting the feeling of being isolated in their classrooms, teachers, particularly those in public school classrooms, experience the greatest burden of anyone working in education. It is teachers who have to cope with growing classes, steadily diminishing budgets, and fewer resources. Administrators can be unsupportive. Teachers are demoralized by the debilitating attitudes of students who don't want to learn or who lack respect for any authority. And people new to teaching have their own set of worries, in addition to being exposed to all these problems.

Class Size

What is the ideal class size? Everyone—teachers, parents and students—agrees that small is better. Smaller classes allow teachers time to attend to problems and to give students individual attention, encouraging individual growth.

Teachers of large classes juggle a great deal of responsibility—and more work than teachers in small classes. To ensure that they can teach the full curriculum and the required skills adequately, they have to keep moving steadily and purposefully onward. These teachers often choose shortcuts to make their workload more bearable. They might assign more independent and group work or ask students to grade each other's papers. With teaching pressures and little time for thorough discussions that invite everyone's input, these teachers find it hard to notice problems in the class.

Budget Cuts

Educators across the country are reporting that education budget cuts at all levels have definitely affected teachers and their morale. How unlike the late 1960s and early '70s when I was given a substantial budget that I considered excessive for my class needs. Not able to spend it all, I asked about adding the leftover money into the following year's allowance. I was told that if I didn't spend the entire amount, it would be given to another teacher who would. Today, however, there is rarely enough money for extra resource people or for anything beyond the bare minimum of supplies. "There is less money to maintain the equipment," says one teacher who suggests that now even field trips are too expensive.

Another teacher confesses that amalgamations of resources and downsizing of staff have led to situations where teachers are asked to "teach things we're not always qualified for or interested in." Addressing students' individual needs becomes increasingly problematic when ever-expanding class enrolment inevitably results in a larger group of students with a wider range of abilities, in addition to the integration of special-needs students who have their own requirements. Augmenting these dilemmas are the warnings of Bernard J. Shapiro, Principal and Vice-Chancellor, McGill University,[1] who predicts that continuing budget cuts will lead not only to declining incomes for teachers, but to neglect of the "frills" such as music and art, burn-out of personnel, and rising drop-out rates.

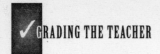

Lack of Time

Time constraints and course loads can easily cause teacher burn-out. Grading work, planning, and preparation for class consume many more hours than actual in-class time. Often, teachers are also expected to volunteer in extra-curricular school activities of one kind or another. Spare moments are at a premium. A separate school teacher in western Canada tells about preparing lesson plans for thirty-six to forty-two classes in a six-day cycle, which means teaching three subjects to twenty-six to thirty-two students in each of seven classes daily. This teacher spends considerable extra time on schoolwork—anywhere from one to two hours per night during the week to five to six hours on weekends. When asked about her ability to handle the numbers of students, the answer is "yes [and] no...it depends on the class—the amount of teachable time disappears quickly if students are not self-controlled and motivated. There are classes I cannot cope with easily. Students often do not ask for help until it is too late for remediation." And it is far more difficult for teachers in large classes to check if everyone understands the concepts taught and is keeping up, or to find any free time to help individual students.

Problem Students

Another common complaint among educators is the large number of students who refuse to learn. Teachers say it is enormously difficult to teach people who are undisciplined, not motivated, disaffected, alienated, and unresponsive. It is also difficult to teach when classes are purposely disrupted by students who just aren't interested in schooling. Teachers don't want to spend their precious instruction time disciplining kids. And it is impossible to teach people who don't come to class regularly, and who do not complete or hand in assignments.

Teachers are also affected by escalating social problems originating outside of the school. Large numbers of children come to class hungry or are having family difficulties and can't concentrate. Dr. Shapiro expresses concern that:

> …[the] major change [in teaching] has been the range of social, emotional, physical and intellectual problems with which an ordinary classroom teacher must deal, often deflecting the major effort from teaching/learning to other matters that must be addressed before students are able to take advantage of instruction. Many schools have become therapy centres and all-purpose institutions with regard to social problems and issues.[2]

Lack of Support

Teachers also bewail the fact that their principals and other administrators do not offer them much-needed support, such as help and encouragement with disciplinary problems or extra resources. Teachers cannot properly do their job if they feel that the principal or

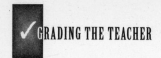

department heads are non-supportive, insensitive to professional requests, and routinely undermine their decisions and authority. They need to feel that the administration supports them and provides them with the appropriate resource personnel. Teachers will soar with leadership that demonstrates a positive attitude and that is open to ideas, allowing time for creativity and encouraging initiative. The best administration is open, honest, and up front with the staff.

The Emotional Nature of the Work

Managing the lives of students can be highly emotional work that drains teachers. A teacher must, indeed, be a juggler every day, balancing the stress of personal and professional demands with that of dealing with a great many individuals and groups of people every day. Classes are filled with students who come from diverse backgrounds and cultures, not all of which are support-ive of the teacher and what he is doing in the class-room. Some teachers compare themselves to parents who are constantly giving, while students are constantly taking. The hardest thing for any teacher to do is to put a foot down and say, "I've given enough and have to take a break." Many teachers emphasize the need for holiday time to relax and unwind. "The stress of [try-ing] to keep kids motivated [combined with the many other demands of teaching] wears me out—I have a life outside school also and my family has needs to be met as well," says a teacher whose view is shared by many of her colleagues. She, like other teachers, looks forward to vacation time, when she plans to "get away as far from teaching as possible [to] wind down—usually camping and working on crafts as well as look[ing] after my home and family which get neglected during the school year." A teacher needs to have space and time to re-energize.

Problems of New Teachers

In addition to the aforementioned pressures, novice teachers face particular challenges. First, the amount of advance preparation, or prep work, is substantial. Every student teacher is warned that the first two or three years of teaching means continual prep work, grading assignments and tests, reading material, and researching and gathering information from all sources.

The physical demands are stressful. It is especially exhausting for a new teacher to mediate, to grade work, to stand up in front of a class talking, and to involve the students in conversation. A lot of new teachers arrive home exhausted every day, drained emotionally, mentally, and physically.

New teachers can experience enormous anxiety. If there is no support system established in the school, the situation becomes increasingly difficult. "You're floating," says new teacher Risa Gitelman. "You figure that everything that's happening in the classroom is only happening to you, and it's all because you're a first-year teacher. You can't believe the amount of work that you're doing and that you're still surviving and that you still have the energy to get up there and teach."

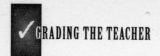

Assessing the Combined Successes

In light of all their responsibilities and stresses, can school teachers adequately address individual student needs? No teachers or administrators give an unqualified yes. Confesses one educator: "It is more difficult to be all things to all students. More support staff are needed. The bright and gifted kids are often shortchanged. Money goes to behavioral and special needs." Some educators are quite adamant in their opinions: "No!" declares a high school principal, while pointing out that we all have differing expectation levels, but "the key word is 'adequately'—if mediocre is sufficient, yes."

So, with all these forces pulling on teachers, especially when the economy worsens, threatening or creating cutbacks of resources and personnel, particularly in the public school system, it is of prime importance that parents be even more vigilant and supportive. The people affected most by upheavals in the educational system are the pupils, our children.

Performance Policies for Teachers

To ensure teachers upgrade their skills and work on their weaknesses, schools and boards have their own performance policies and processes for teacher evaluation. For instance, a Winnipeg board requires mandatory evaluation of tenured teachers every three years. New teachers are evaluated every three months during the first year and then either tenured or released.

An example of a program that keeps track of its

teachers' performance progress is the one offered by the North York Board of Education. Each year all its teachers are required to file what the board refers to as the "Supervision for Growth Plan," which outlines the professional growth activities they will participate in during the following year. The activities might include registering for courses to upgrade their skills or degrees, to expand their knowledge in specific areas, or to work towards moving into the administrative track. Writing books, attending conferences, exploring more effective ways to teach such topics as quadratic equations, for example, or becoming computer literate are other ways teachers might develop themselves. Furthermore, individual and staff professional growth plans must bear a relationship to the school's mandate, which is reviewed every three years (its objectives are shared with the community through newsletters and meetings). Among the priorities a school could adopt might be improving math skills and literacy or addressing race relations.

Annually, each and every staff member discusses his or her "Supervision for Growth Plan" with the principal or vice-principal of the school. It is at this point that a principal might suggest to a particular teacher a line of action specific to the individual's personal professional development.

A second method of supervision, called the "Administrative Track"—a plan for professional development that is directed by administration, rather than voluntary—is an additional step that can be taken if a teacher is not keeping up to date. Involving formal

classroom inspection and more direction from the principal, the process can be threatening if a teacher feels forced into it. On the other hand, teachers can also opt for the "Administrative Track" if they are seeking promotion, if they want to have some directed guidance about how their professional career is progressing, or if they intend to change boards and would like an up-to-date written recommendation.

When a person is studied for serious evaluation with possibility of termination, a third level, used infrequently in the case of tenured teachers but more often than people think, is the "Performance Review Track." Teachers start off as probationary teachers. The probationary period offers the opportunity for administration to let go teachers whose performance is not satisfactory. Teachers in the probationary period might be on the regular "Supervision for Growth Plan," but they're all on the "Administrative Track" until their probationary period is finished.

Help Available for Teachers

Today, in spite of spending cutbacks, there is still a range of support systems through which school administrations offer guidance, support, and resources to teachers.

School Specialists

All boards have resource personnel to assist teachers. In one New Brunswick school board, a teacher can apply for help from an "R and M" (Resource and Methods) teacher, a mentor, teachers' aides, the librarian, as well as a guidance counsellor. Another school board tries to ensure that each school has program leaders and/or consultants in all of the subject areas and at all levels. Any teacher can ask for assistance from one of the board staff who specializes in the teacher's field. A principal might also suggest, "I think we should have the history consultant in to talk to you about the new program in Black Studies that you're working on."

Community Resources

Teachers can also count on community resources, some of which are the school, public and university libraries, the board resource centre, art galleries, museums, and heritage programs. Traditional service industries, which include police and fire departments, are other resources. As well, teachers can turn to specialists in the community, whether business people or parents who are professionals or entrepreneurs in business and manufacturing. Often those who dedicate themselves to the arts—visual artists, writers, musicians, actors, and playwrights—offer themselves to schools, either for free or with a grant of government money, to perform or teach their skills at schools.

Classes and Workshops

Although they usually cost money (unless the school or board provides funding), teachers can also make use of continuing education courses and summer institutes. Specialization certificates for teachers are offered in dozens of diverse courses in such areas as Language Arts, Remediation, ESL, School Librarianship, Special Education (based on understanding the needs of individual students), and Teaching the Deaf and Hard of Hearing.

Thornhill, Ontario, professional artist and art teacher Elaine Clarfield-Gitalis says that, for her, teaching and attending workshops are ongoing learning processes: "In life there's always more to know; one can never know enough." She frequently participates in workshops led by people she feels are more experienced than she is so that she can glean from them information and knowledge which she first analyzes and then gives back to her students. In addition to using her own personal experiences in teaching, she draws upon the theoretical and technical information found in her main resources: art books and magazines about and/or written by artists. She views each book as a culmination of its author's experience and knowledge. As a result, besides using them as wells of information for herself, she regularly recommends books to her students.

Many teachers use after-school and holiday time to upgrade their qualifications. After graduating from teacher's college, Marilyn Matthews, a New Brunswick junior high school teacher, went on to complete separate education and sociology degrees at the University of New Brunswick, a Master's degree in Education at the University of Moncton (where she also took French studies), and her Special Education diploma at McGill University.

Professional Development Days

Professional development (PD) days (or Professional Activity Days) are set aside by the board to focus on topical issues and also to educate the teachers, making them aware of problems and helping them find solutions. Staffs get together and decide what issue(s) they need to highlight. For example, a school that has been having problems with student violence might invite consultants to talk about conflict-resolution strategies. Another school whose PD day centres entirely on sexual harassment—of students by teachers or by other students—defines harassment so that teachers learn to identify and understand the issue, and become sensitized enough to stop or prevent any behaviour they now know is inappropriate.

Students

Many teachers are adamant about the fact that their own students are a great resource. They bring into the class refreshing opinions and new and unusual ways of perceiving the world and resolving its challenges. Teachers often say that their students teach them. For instance, sometimes, when students say, "I tried this, and it really worked for me," teachers find a great new approach.

The process of teaching is a learning experience in another way. By developing lessons that address the needs of the collective class as well as its individuals, the teacher can learn a great deal about the subject, and herself, particularly how far she can stretch as a professional.

The process can also open new avenues for her, whether it has to do with a new piece of knowledge, another way of thinking or approach, or some personal gain. Elaine Clarfield-Gitalis once taught an exercise in which everyone had to first mix up a black paint and then create a silhouette on an interesting background. Developing that lesson gave her the idea for what she regards as the most successful painting in her next show; she acknowledges she would never have produced the painting if she hadn't been creating the lesson for her students.

Colleagues

Principals can create situations in which teachers work together, learning from each other's strengths. Regular meetings of the staff also provide the opportunity to talk about students and programs and, possibly, the ways in which they can teach together. At these gatherings, teachers can help each other in a variety of ways, sharing ideas, experiences, resources, lesson plans, and educational materials they have created.

Mentoring

One support system for teachers is "mentoring." A principal who knows that teacher A has strengths in a particular area in which teacher B is lacking arranges that the teachers will spend some time together, helping each other. Another mentoring arrangement occurs when a consultant, department head, vice-principal, or principal offers or agrees to guide a teacher along in his or her career. Furthermore, teachers can meet with any of these people to discuss isolated or ongoing situations when they occur and to brainstorm solutions. Two teachers might even schedule time to assist or observe in one another's classrooms. Team teaching is yet another possibility where individuals can learn from each other. Teachers who team teach plan the curriculum and timetabling together, splitting the classes and subjects among themselves.

In their dealings with teachers, parents should take into consideration the strains and stresses that teachers encounter daily. Parents might also want to check the possible resources and programs for teachers available at their school or board. If there is no established policy about teacher support and upgrading, perhaps through a parents' group parents can help institute one.

CHAPTER EIGHT

The Roles and Responsibilities of Principals and Bureaucrats

I have to answer to the parents...to my staff and...to the kids in a way. So I'd better be careful what my decisions are. I am the person at the top, so to speak, but I do have to answer to a lot of people.

—Dalia Eisen, director of Crestwood School

The key administrator of each school, whether a headmaster, director, co-ordinator, or principal, sets the tone of the school. How good this administrator is can have a great deal to do with how good the school is. Without doubt, the chief administrator's attitudes and professionalism have a trickle-down effect to the members on the staff.

A good school administrator has many qualities. She is well organized and efficient. She walks the fine line between satisfying the needs of the staff and those of the students. Making herself easily available to staff, students and parents, she demonstrates respect for everyone in each group. She addresses the issues they raise and deals with them. A good arbitrator, she sympathizes with all sides. She demonstrates a keen aptitude for comprehending the crux of a problem and then resolving it. She has the ability not only to work out solutions but also to act on them. She tries to ensure that she leaves no issue dangling unfinished or problem unresolved.

The principal plays many roles in relation to the staff, students, parents, and community at large.

Roles of the Principal

A principal balances a multitude of responsibilities within the school. Generally, the principal is expected to provide strong, productive leadership to the school community, use diplomacy in dealing with staff, students, and parents, and develop a spirit of togetherness and mutual goodwill with staff and students.

A longtime principal says he functions in the role of educational leader, which breaks down into four separate yet overlapping components: 1) administration, 2) planning, 3) developing the curriculum, and 4) community relations.

1) THE ADMINISTRATOR

The administrator is in charge of the day-to-day functioning of the building. Not only does he supervise the people and programs, he also oversees the upkeep of the "plant," or physical building itself, and its grounds.

2) THE PLANNER

As the planner, the principal determines where the school is going in the future, setting the example and standard. In planning overall school agendas and policies, principals offer guidance in the creation of long- and short-term goals in addition to developing the strategies to accomplish those goals. Good principals call upon their staff and parent community to give their input in the planning and decision-making.

Public school principals are often required to take part in out-of-school committees. Since they are familiar with all the system's rules and processes, experienced principals are pulled out of the school more often than they would like in order to participate on committees for the board. At these times, they work on overall policy ideas dealing with such issues as teacher evaluation, peer mentoring, and staffing procedures.

3) CURRICULUM LEADER

With ultimate responsibility for curriculum development and implementation, the principal oversees the departments, grades, classes, and individual teachers.

In the role of curriculum leader the principal instructs and hires the staff and also organizes the structure of the school in such a way as to take advantage of the staff's strengths. The principal identifies each teacher's weaknesses or deficiencies and guides teachers towards improvement.

Although the principal is one of the most important factors in what the school is like, that shouldn't be taken to mean that his ideas are shared by everyone in the building. He encourages the staff to come along with him. And if the staff members have been with the school long before the principal got there, they don't always follow his lead; some of them go ahead as they've always done. In some cases, that's just fine. But, as several principals point out, when the teachers' ideas are quite different from the principal's, especially in the area of school philosophy, it can lead to a difficult and uneasy school environment. Some principals might disagree absolutely with almost everything certain teachers do educationally, and yet these teachers will be very highly thought of by the parents and considered the best in the school.

In order to operate together as a team, the principal and the teachers have to compromise. As well, if the principal is wishy-washy, weak, misdirected, or unresponsive, then the staff members (collectively or individually) will have to either adopt his attitude or take matters into their own hands. If the staff respects him, however, the school will tend to reflect his philosophies and premises. For example, if the principal believes that parent involvement is important and welcome, he will try to ensure that the office and staff adopt an open-door school policy. Setting the precedent, he opens his office and the school to receive parents at any time. He welcomes parents in, introduces them to the staff, and encourages their participation in the school. By making them feel comfortable and part of the education process, the principal demonstrates that he appreciates their suggestions and input.

4) COMMUNICATIONS OFFICER

The principal is the school's liaison to the outside world, responding to the criticisms and/or demands of their students' parents while simultaneously promoting the school to the best of his or her abilities. While reporting to their school boards, principals are also directly accountable to the parents (who let them know if they have concerns), to the staff (who can be quite critical), to the kids (who, at times, can have plenty to say), and to some degree to their superintendents (who are the agents of the boards).

Hiring Teachers

A principal can shape the direction of the school when she hires teachers to fill available positions. Even if the position is temporary, who the principal and her hiring committee employ often sends an important message to the other teachers about the direction in which the principal would like to see the school go.

Evaluation

Typically, if he is notified by others or suspects that a teacher is deficient or needs guidance, the principal might make a point of visiting the classroom daily to observe the class in progress. If he feels a teacher is not having success in a particular area, as part of the process for improvement he might suggest that that teacher take a course in whatever the weakness is. If you want to know if teachers in your school are regularly evaluated and, if so, how, ask your principal.

Disciplining Teachers

Depending on the teacher's level of incompetence or transgression, the steps principals take to discipline teachers range anywhere from a reprimand or a letter of warning all the way up to suspension and dismissal by the board. Usually, a principal can give "official warnings" for late arrivals, not carrying out supervision, ignoring directives, inappropriate behaviour towards children (such as excessive screaming or bullying). The principal might also try to provide supports, such as experts and mentors, or even change the teacher's assignments within the school.

But teachers cannot be *forced* to upgrade their skills, knowledge, and/or manner of approach; they don't *have* to change. If the teacher resists change or upgrading, what options are available to public school administrators? District supervisory staff can be brought in. The union can be consulted. A negative report can be written, documenting instances of incompetency and, if need be, recommending that the board dismiss the teacher. Each private school has its own procedures to follow if there is a problem with or grievance against a teacher. However, since teachers' security in private schools is tenuous—they might not be represented by a union, and their contracts or commitments are usually renewed annually—they can be let go much more easily than those in the public system.

Moving Teachers

A continually frustrating situation for principals is that

they can't respond adequately to the racial and ethnic make-up of the population. Instead, as neighbourhoods change, the teachers tend to remain, and it's very difficult to hire new teachers to reflect the change. Even if a board attempts to target the hiring of particular minority groups reflective of those in the school community, most of the teachers might also be new to teaching, and would be at risk for being laid off.

Because of their collective agreements, the boards must accommodate teachers with seniority. When staff must be cut, it is those who have worked the longest who have priority, regardless of their qualifications: a two-year teacher who is brilliant in her job will be let go before the twenty-year veteran who is tired, boring, and not stimulating. Further staffing problems are created within school boards whose growth is static. With no new positions opening up, tenured teachers have little opportunity to move to new positions and new schools. So even if the principal or the teacher feels a move is appropriate, it might be impossible.

Principals do try to "weed out" ineffective or bad teachers. Sometimes, as drastic and unfair as it may seem, it is simply easier for a principal to just pass on a problem teacher to another school: the teacher in question is either persuaded (gently or sometimes by being made to feel very uncomfortable in the working environment) to apply to another school or board or is given a glowing but fraudulent endorsement by the first school's administration. One principal I know says she tries to remove and replace one such teacher a year.

If conditions seem to warrant it, she also tries to "persuade" others to take a leave of absence for sickness or mental health reasons. Another principal deliberately makes such demands upon his staff that those who do not agree with his values or attitude leave on their own: then he has the opportunity to replace them.

The bottom line is that the individual cannot be made to leave, and in all likelihood the principal will move on before the teacher. Principals and vice-principals, especially in the public system, are moved around from school to school. Good ones and bad ones come and go. Length of tenure varies from situation to situation but commonly lasts from three to five years. A good principal often *wants* different experiences because he enjoys the chance to get into new situations and work out solutions every few years. Many teachers feel this way, too: they don't like to stay in the same school or grade forever.

Firing

After attempts at change have failed, opportunities to get rid of the teacher are slim, but it's not impossible. In the public school system, once a teacher is hired on a permanent contract, it is difficult for a board to fire her without going through all the steps outlined in the contract or collective agreements. And, as one school board trustee confided, too many incompetent teachers have redeeming qualities that prevent them from being removed, even when remediation has not been successful. Andrew Nikiforuk, in his book *School's Out*, claims that:

> Bad teachers are notoriously difficult to get
> rid of. Instead of firing people who can't
> teach, the system either promotes or recycles
> them. Most trades or professions routinely
> dismiss 5 percent of their members as incom-
> petents. In teaching, the average rate of dis-
> missal is .05 [percent]. The reluctance of
> unions to prepare bad teachers for other lines
> of work is an abuse of children and an insult
> to good teachers.[1]

Public school teachers can be fired for documented
incompetence, sexual or physical abuse. If a public
school teacher is considered incompetent, the principal
can start a process for removal as outlined in school or
board policy procedures. The process itself can be long,
complicated, and tedious, and it's not always successful.
There are no individual contracts for public school
teachers, only the collective agreements, negotiated
with the boards through the teachers' unions. A principal would have to follow the terms of the agreement to
the letter, document everything, and seek the advice of
supervisors. Part of the process might include notifying
the teacher verbally or writing an official note or a
memo that the teacher would be asked to sign.

In the public system, only boards can fire teachers,
but principals can make recommendations to the
boards for dismissal. Principals in private schools have

more direct authority. Crestwood School director Dalia Eisen points out that she doesn't have written contracts:

> If a teacher insists on one, I will do it, [but] it's not worth the paper it's written on. If that teacher wants to pick up [midway through the year] and leave me, there's not a thing I can do about it. And if I had a teacher here who had a written contract and hit a child, contract or no contract, [he'd] be gone, I don't care what that piece of paper said.

All the principals I interviewed say that they have sometimes encountered teachers who are incompetent but have rarely, if ever, met teachers who are physically, psychologically, or sexually abusive to children. If, however, teachers were identified as possible alcoholics or as having psychological problems, how would they be addressed? One principal I spoke to says he would first seek the advice of his supervisor and of his union to help him work out a joint strategy. Another principal says that formally she'd first discuss the situation as she saw it with the teacher, then she'd provide options and support, and, finally, she'd notify the supervisor and human resources personnel. In addition she'd informally network with colleagues and offer the teacher a short-term reduced workload and counselling.

What disciplinary procedures against abusive teachers are available to principals and other administrators?

If immediate action is necessary, administration advises the board office and starts the paperwork to suspend the teacher. A teacher's gross misconduct and/or unethical behaviour can lead to immediate dismissal.

Students and the Principal

The position of principal is one of the few in the school system, besides that of teacher, that allows someone to have a direct influence on students. Good principals are sympathetic to students; they try to acknowledge, honour, and administer to each student's educational needs and concerns. Many principals try to keep their teaching skills honed so they squeeze time in to teach some classes, too. Some principals I know try to learn their students' names in order to address them personally. Principals also move around the school, making impromptu visits to the classes. To some degree, visiting classrooms allows the principals to monitor the curriculum and how it is being taught. This "hands on" approach also keeps them in touch with the students as well as the staff.

Parents and the Principal

One of the key factors of a principal's job is dealing with parents. That interaction, which may be on either an individual or group basis, entails talking and listening to parents and solving their school-related problems. It also includes familiarizing parents not only with school and board procedures but also with the jargon common to education.

By informing parents of their vital role in their children's education, educational administrators can give mothers and fathers tools to better fulfil that role. Good principals encourage parents to join or form parent associations, knowing that in order for any parent group to be successful, it is essential that school administration be supportive. Maybelle Durkin, CHSPTF executive director, most definitely insists that "a parent body [can't] exist in the school unless the principal approves and assists; otherwise he or she can make it horrendous—not by working against it, but by simply doing nothing—by not communicating to the public at all."

Most principals understand what the schools can do and how the system works. As a result, there are some built-in frustrations when parents demand actions or results that principals just know they're not going to be able to deliver. They have to live with the knowledge that sometimes problems are not going to be solved. In fact, principals cannot be successful all the time. Why? Because all of those other groups they're dealing with aren't all infallible. Parents aren't all perfect; they don't all necessarily have a good fix on what their kids' problems are. Other times, the kids themselves go their own way, no matter what help anyone gives them. And sometimes teachers and principals will never see eye to eye, and teachers stubbornly take their own path.

There is no doubt that any good principal must adapt almost daily to deal with unexpected school-related incidents, crises, and demands. Simultaneously, she must be a proficient juggler, tending to her manifold regular responsibilities while trying to develop or maintain an open, friendly school environment that is highly conducive both to teaching and to learning. All the principal needs to be successful in her endeavours is the combined goodwill, determined efforts, and hard work of staff, students, and parents.

Conclusion

One of the most important jobs that parents take on is supervising the education of their children. The formal education itself is a job that the majority of us have turned over to our private or public schools. We entrust the educators in those institutions with teaching our children in accordance with the beliefs that we uphold and the priorities we have established.

Most parents care deeply about the quality of their children's education, but too many are hesitant or reluctant to become involved. Perhaps they feel powerless in the face of what seems to have become a huge and overwhelmingly bureaucratic system; perhaps they feel unqualified to judge teachers and administrators who they consider specially qualified professional educators.

Whatever the case, it is time for parents to assert themselves and make a difference in the school system. While the primary interest of everybody involved in the education of children is to help each child be as successful as possible, there are times when it may be necessary for the parent to act as the child's special advocate. *Grading the Teacher* was written to encourage parents to take on that role, and to give them the tools to accomplish it as effectively as possible.

Take the information offered in this book and get to know your school: its goals and missions; the quality of its administration; its ability to meet your child's individual needs. Most of all, take a long, discerning, and understanding look at your child's teachers. The fate of your child's success in education lies in their hands. How is their behaviour affecting your child's behaviour and learning? Using the approaches outlined here, reinforce the positive influences and take steps to improve the negative.

If you can, go that one step further and get involved in education at the policy-making level as well, through parent-teacher groups or advisory committees. It is up to parents to make sure that their voices are heard when the goals of our schools and the methods they use to encourage our children's learning are being decided. It's up to you to make the difference.

Notes

Introduction

[1] Heather Robertson, "Deciding your child's future," *Toronto Life*, September 1992.

[2] Roberta Israeloff, "Special Education Report," *Parents* magazine, October 1992.

[3] Otherwise known as the Family of Schools. In my area, this includes all the elementary, junior high, and high schools within a specified district.

Chapter One—A Good School

[1] Michelle Landsberg, "A Right-wing Attack on our Public Schools," *The Toronto Star*, 9 September 1995.

[2] Andrew Nikiforuk, *If Learning Is So Natural, Why Am I Going to School?* (Toronto: Penguin Books Canada, 1994), p. 85.

Chapter Two—Recognizing Good Teaching

[1] Fred Rogers, quoted in Anne Hillerman, "Teacher, Teacher," *Mothering* magazine, Spring Issue 1992, p. 112.

[2] Kevin Leman, *Growing Up Firstborn* (New York: Dell Publishing, 1989), pp. 281-82.

[3] Mark H. McCormack, *What They Don't Teach You at*

Harvard Business School (New York: Bantam Books, 1986), p. 36.

4 Wess Roberts, *Straight A's Never Made Anybody Rich* (New York: HarperCollins Publishers, 1991), p. 22.

5 Richard D. Lavoie, *How Difficult Can This Be?* (Greenwich, CT: F.A.T. City Workshop, Eagle High School OUTREACH).

6 Nita Leland, *Creative Artist* (Cincinnati, Ohio: Writer's Digest Books, 1990).

7 A written outline of the teacher's expectations might help circumvent misunderstandings, as well. If a teacher indicates that her grading will be based mainly on the depth of research and collection of material, she cannot after the fact choose to focus on form and presentation. The written outline thus not only provides a concrete plan for the student to follow, but also gives him recourse for appeal, if need be.

8 Ann Landers, column in the *Toronto Star*, 4 February 1993.

9 Gloria Steinem, *Revolution From Within* (Toronto: Little, Brown and Company (Canada) Limited, 1992), p. 13.

Chapter Three—The Evidence

1 Gerald Owen, "Ship of Schools: A Special Report on Education," *Homemaker's Magazine*, September 1992.

2 Richard D. Lavoie, *How Difficult Can This Be?* (Greenwich, CT: F.A.T. City Workshop, Eagle High School OUTREACH).

[3] Ann Druyan, quoted in, "On the trail of the meaning of life," *The Toronto Star*, 28 November 1992.

[4] Wess Roberts, *Straight A's Never Made Anybody Rich* (New York: HarperCollins Publishers, 1991), p. 109.

[5] Judy Barron and Sean Barron, *There's A Boy in Here* (New York: Simon and Schuster, 1992), p. 260.

Chapter Four—Evaluating the Teacher

[1] Jennifer Lewington and Graham Orpwood, *Overdue Assignment, Taking Responsibility for Canada's Schools* (Etobicoke, Ontario: John Wiley & Sons Canada Limited, 1995), p. 43.

[2] Tom Fennel, "Some universities are placing new emphasis on their professors' work in the classroom," in "Special Report: Teaching Class," *Maclean's*, 9 November 1992, p. 56.

Chapter Five—Making Changes

[1] Gerald Owen, "Ship of Schools," *Homemaker's Magazine*, September 1992.

[2] The Ontario Ministry of Education condensed "Provincial Review Report on Alternative Schools and Programs in the Public System (1986)."

[3] Francesca Piredda, *Report to Parents*, Ontario Ministry of Education and Training, February 1994.

Chapter Six—Understanding the Roles and Responsibilities of Students and Parents

[1] Apparently the Calgary Council of Home and School Associations has 18,000 volunteers in schools.

[2] Jennifer Lewington and Graham Orpwood, *Overdue Assignment, Taking Responsibility for Canada's Schools* (Etobicoke, Ontario: John Wiley & Sons Canada Limited, 1995), p. 267.

[3] Gerald Owen, "Ship of Schools, A Special Report on Education," *Homemaker's Magazine*, September 1992.

Chapter Seven—Understanding Teachers

[1] Bernard J. Shapiro is a former professor of Education and Public Policy at the University of Toronto, deputy minister of Colleges and Universities, Ontario, and deputy minister of Education, Ontario. The statement is from a letter to the author.

[2] Bernard J. Shapiro, from a letter to the author.

Chapter Eight—The Roles and Responsibilities of Principals and Bureaucrats

1 Andrew Nikiforuk, *School's Out* (Toronto: Macfarlane Walter & Ross, 1993), p. 113.

Appendix

A. *Parent Associations*

To network with parent groups in the wider community or for further information contact the parent-teacher association at your school and/or any of the following parents' organizations and associations.

THE ONTARIO PARENT COUNCIL

56 Wellesley St. W., 16th floor
Toronto, ON
M7A 2B7
Phone: 416 314-0427 or 1-800-361-6483 Fax: 416 314-0425
(Contact your provincial education ministry—listed at the end of the appendix—for information about parent councils in your province or territory)

THE CANADIAN HOME AND SCHOOL AND PARENT-TEACHER FEDERATION (CHSPTF)

Suite 104-858 Bank St.
Ottawa, ON
K1S 3W3
Phone: 613 234-7292 Fax: 613 234-3913
Maybelle Durkin, Executive Director

CHSPTF PROVINCIAL AFFILIATES:

British Columbia Confederation of Parent Advisory
Councils
1540-1185 West Georgia St.
Vancouver, BC
V6E 4E6
Phone: 604 687-4433 Fax: 604 687-4488

Alberta Home and School Councils' Association
12310-105 Avenue N.W., Suite 102
Edmonton, AB
T5N 0Y4
Toll-free phone: 1-800-661-3470

Saskatchewan Federation of Home and School
Associations
221 Cumberland Ave. N.
Saskatoon, SK
S7N 1M3
Phone/fax: 306 955-5723

Manitoba Association of Parent Councils
Room 309, 1181 Portage Ave.
Winnipeg, MB
R3G 0T3
Phone: 204 786-4722 Fax: 204 774-8553

Ontario Federation of Home and School Associations
Incorporated
252 Bloor St.W. Suite 12-200
Toronto, ON
M5S 1V5
Phone: 416 924-7491 Fax: 416 924-5354

Quebec Federation of Home and School Associations
3285 Cavendish Blvd., Suite 562
Montreal, PQ
H4B 2L9
Phone/fax: 514 481-5619

New Brunswick Federation of Home and School
Associations, Inc.
R.R.#1, Box 367
Scoudouc, NB
E0A 1N0
Phone: 506 532-6775

Nova Scotia Federation of Home and School
Associations
P.O. Box 578
Halifax, Nova Scotia
B3J 2S9

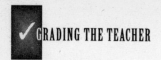

Prince Edward Island Home and School Federation
P.O. Box 1012 (3 Queen St.)
Charlottetown, PEI
C1A 7M4
Phone: 902 892-0664 Fax: 902 368-4548

Newfoundland and Labrador Home and School
Federation
P.O. Box 23140, 5 Merrymeeting Rd.
St. John's, NF
A1B 4J9
Phone: 709 739-4830 Fax: 709 739-4833

B. Advocacy Groups

The following are advocacy groups working towards improving education. Join one, or start your own.

COALITION FOR EDUCATION REFORM

81 Sciberras Rd.
Unionville, ON
L3R 2J5
905 477-5397

COALITION FOR EDUCATION REFORM MEMBER GROUPS:

Some of the Coalition for Education Reform member groups are as follows. For a full list, contact the Coalition for Education Reform.

Educators' Association for Quality Education
81 Sciberras Rd.
Unionville, ON
L3R 2J5
*(An organization of teachers and other school support per-
sonnel dedicated to accountability and effectiveness in
Ontario public education.)*

Ontario School Board Reform Network (OSBRN)
16 Simonston Blvd.
Thornhill, ON
L3T 4L1
*(A coalition of individual reform-minded trustees and
concerned taxpayers.)*

Parents in Action
135 Centennial Drive
Port Hope, ON
L1A 3X6
*(Citizens determined to see change in Ontario's education
system.)*

The Organization for Quality Education (OQE)
170 University Avenue W., Suite 12-218
Waterloo, ON
N2L 3E9
905 477-5397
Internet: http://www.hookup.net/~dare

OQE Provincial Contacts:

ALBERTA
Grant Sikstrom
68 Akins Drive,
St. Alberta, AB
T8N 2Y7
403 459-8692

BRITISH COLUMBIA
John Pippus
13494 18th Ave.
Surrey, BC
V4A 1W3
604 538-7438

MANITOBA
Alice Little
511-55 Garry
Winnipeg, MB
R3C 4H4
204 957-5518

NEW BRUNSWICK
Beth Buerkle
R.R. #2
St. Andrews, NB
E0G 2X0
506 529-4382

NEWFOUNDLAND
Jim Hornell
15 Gardener St.
Grand Falls/Windsor, NF
A2A 2T3
709 489-7538

NOVA SCOTIA
Jenny White
R.R. 3, Centreville
King's County, NS
B0P 1J0
902 679-5600

ONTARIO (Regional Contacts)

Brant: Debbie Andre	519 448-1889
Dufferin: Rick Middlebrook	519 942-0245
Durham: Patti Charbonneau	905 286-2984
East York: Debbie Drainie	416 755-2447
Elgin: Kathy Cronheimer	519 633-7587
Essex: Robert Cartlidge	519 326-2687
Frontenac/Kingston: Lisa Moses	613 335-2001
Grey: Irene and Dave Ward	519 371-5069
Halton: Jennifer Brooks	905 827 8611
Hamilton/Wentworth:	
Nancy Freckleton	905 628-4198
Hastings/Prince Edward: Ted Johnson	613 395-3990
Kenora: Wanda Raymond	807 468-5652
Lakehead: Lori Paterson	807 768-1003

Lambton: Allan McKeown   519 542-3661
London: Craig Stevens   519 473-0802
London/Middlesex Separate: H. Bos   519 473-2078
Middlesex Public: Judy Sumner   519 666-0809
Niagara: Vic Mamchych   905 384-2293
Nipissing (North Bay): Ann Fudge   705 472-5602
Nipissing (Sudbury): Lynda Olsen   705 523-0840
North York: Julie Wood   416 638-7595
North/Newcastle: Cindy Chatterson   905 885-2028
Ottawa: Theresa Ziebell   613 722-1693
Oxford: Kathy Lubitz   519 684-7686
Parry Sound: Christina Dowell   705 342-5502
Peel: Elizabeth Beadon   519 941-6137
Peterborough: Maureen Somers   705 939-2035
Scarborough: Steve Swigger   416 499-8706
Simcoe (Barrie): Wendy Cahill   705 734-2602
Simcoe (Wasaga Beach): L. Matthews   705 429-1155
Toronto: Sydney MacInnis   416 489-9402
Toronto French: Mireille Bealle   416 493-9014
Waterloo: Karen Mitchell   519 725-5420
Wellington: John Akin   519 836-2965
Windsor: Beth Cooper   519 966-4114
York Region North: Bill Everitt   905 836-0533
York Region South: Rita Kavanagh   905 477-5397

C. Publications:

1. GENERAL EDUCATION

Home And School, Canada's Education Magazine, 105 West Beaver Creek, Unit 2, Richmond Hill, Ontario, L4B 1C6
Phone: 905 886-1212 Fax: 905-886-6868.

Forum (quarterly newsletter with annual membership to the Organization for Quality Education, $15.00), OQE, 170 University Avenue W., Suite 12-218, Waterloo, Ontario, N2L 3E9
Malkin Dare, editor: 519 884-3166.

Could do Better. What's Wrong with Public Education in Ontario and How to Fix It. A report on Ontario's Public Education System, by The Coalition for Education Reform. 81 Sciberras Rd., Unionville, Ontario, L3R 2J5. (Appendix C consists of a broad list of sources and further reading.)

2. PUBLIC AND PRIVATE SCHOOLS AND SCHOOL BOARDS

MDR's Canadian School Directory 1995 is a comprehensive guide listing names, addresses, telephone and fax numbers of every school and school board in Canada, current names and job titles of principals, board administrators, and key consultants, as well as total number of schools in each board with school enrollments and grade spans. If the local school board or library does not have a copy and you would like to

either locate or buy one ($94.95), contact the Canadian
Education Association, 252 Bloor St. W., Suite 8-200,
Toronto, Ontario, M5S 1V5. Phone: 416 924-7721
Fax: 416 924-3188

Nowers, Beth, and Bell, Jennifer. *The Good School Book.*
Toronto: Key Porter Books, 1993. A guide to private
education in Canada.

3. CHARTER SCHOOLS:

The matter of charter schools is extensively featured in
the March 1996 issue of *Forum* (volume 4, number 4),
a quarterly newsletter published by the Organization
for Quality Education, 170 University Ave. W., Suite
12-218, Waterloo, Ontario, N2L 3E9
Phone: 905 477-5397.
Internet: http://www.hookup.net/~dare

The Charter School Idea is a 56-minute VHS videotape
program and 112-page book which explains and ana-
lyzes "A Plain Language Review of the Autonomous
School Concept—A new Direction for Public
Education." Available from the Society of Advancing
Educational Research, 57 Allan Close, Red Deer,
Alberta, T4R 1A4
Fax: 403 343-7042. ($24.95 standard order)

For considerable information and printed material about
charter schools, contact also Ron Babiuk, Education
Manager, Charter Schools, Alberta Education,

Edmonton Regional Office, 3rd floor, 11160 Jasper
Avenue, Edmonton, Alberta, T5K 0L2
Phone: 403 427-7484 Fax: 403 422-9682

4. HOME SCHOOLING NETWORKS AND PUBLICATIONS:

For an extensive directory of home-schoolers across
Canada and for what she refers to as "unschooling"
information, contact Wendy Priesnitz, The Canadian
Alliance of Home Schoolers, 272 Hwy. #5, RR #1, St.
George, Ontario, N0E 1N0.
Phone/Fax: 519 448-4001
E-mail: altpress@netroute.net.
Web site: http://www.netroute.net/~altpress/ds/cahs.html

Ray, Dr. Brian D. *A Nationwide Study of Home
Education in Canada: Family Characteristics, Student
Achievement, and other Topics* ($15.00), National Home
Education Research Institute, Western Baptist College,
5000 Deer Park Drive, S.E., Salem, Oregon 97301,
USA.

The *Home School Guide and Directory for Alberta*, compiled by Gayle Crouser, deals with such topics as choosing the right curriculum and planning the school year,
and includes lists of resources, suppliers, support services, periodicals, and major publishers in Canada.
Contact Gayle Crouser, 229 Woodrow Place, Okotoks,
Alberta, T0L 1T5.

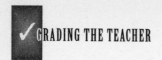

School Free, The Canadian Home School Handbook, by Wendy Priesnitz, covers such topics as legalities, dealing with school officials, guiding self-directed learning, writing a child-based curriculum, developing assessment procedures, and much more. The book is available from The Alternate Press, 272 Hwy. 5, RR 1, St George, Ontario, N0E 1N0. ($16.95).

On the Internet, refer to the Homeschool Resource Page whose Table of Contents includes information from the provinces and territories as well as Canadian books, catalogues and resources, and a list of universities accepting home schoolers: http://www.flora. ottawa.on.ca/homeschool-ca/

Homeschooler's Organization List, compiled by Cindy Lee Duckert on the Internet, provides over 200 pages of names of home-school contacts throughout North America.
http://www.alumni.caltech.edu/~casner/statelist.html

C. Administrators' Associations

Canadian Association of Principals
1010 Polytek Court, Unit 36B
Gloucester, ON
K1J 9J2
Phone: 613 745 8472 Fax: 613 745 6325

D. Provincial Ministries of Education:

British Columbia:
Ministry of Education
Parliament Buildings
Victoria, BC
V8V 2M4
604 387-4611

Alberta:
Ministry of Education
West Tower, Devonian Building
11160 Jasper Ave.
Edmonton, AB
T5K 0L2
403 427-2025

Saskatchewan:
Ministry of Education
2220 College Avenue
Regina, SK
S4P 2V7
306 787-7360

Manitoba:
Department of Education and Training
Legislative Building
Winnipeg, MB
R3C 0V9
204 945-2211

Ontario:
Ministry of Education and Training
Mowat Block, 900 Bay St.
Toronto, ON
M7A 1L2
1-800-387-5514 (toll-free in Ontario)
416-325-2600

Quebec:
Ministère de l'Education
Edifice Marie-Guyart
1035, rue de la Chevrotière
Québec, PQ
G1R 5A5
418 643-7095

New Brunswick:
Department of Education
P.O. Box 6000
Fredericton, NB
E3B 5H1
506 453-3678

Prince Edward Island:
Department of Education
Box 2000
Shaw Building, 4th Floor, 95 Rochford St.
Charlottetown, PE
C1A 7N8
902 368-4600

Nova Scotia:
Department of Education
Box 578
Halifax, NS
B3J 2S9
902 424-5605

Newfoundland:
Department of Education
Box 8700
St. John's, NF
A1B 4J6
709 729-2466

Northwest Territories:
Department of Education, Culture and Employment
Programs
P.O. Box 1320
Yellowknife, NT
X1A 2L9
403 873-7529

Yukon:
Department of Education
P.O. Box 2703
Whitehorse, YT
Y1A 2C6
403 667-5141

Bibliography

Some of the following eclectic readings focus on education issues entirely, others just touch upon them, but all
consider in significant ways some of the themes of
teaching, learning, or development of self-esteem.

Books

Alexiou, Chris. *Starting Small: Thinking Big, Practical
Strategies for School Success.* Oakville, Ontario: Mosaic
Press, 1995.

Barron, Judy, and Barron, Sean. *There's a Boy in Here.*
New York: Simon & Schuster, 1992.

Coleman, Peter. *Learning About Schools: What Parents
Need to Know and How They Can Find Out.*
Montréal: Institute for Research and Public Policy,
1994.

Conway, Jill Ker. *The Road From Coorain.* New York:
First Vintage Books, Random House, 1990.

Dixon, Des R. G. *Future Schools.* Toronto: ECW Press,
1992.

Dryden, Ken. *In School: Our Kids, Our Teachers, Our
Classrooms.* Toronto: McClelland & Stewart Inc.,
1995.

Fry, Ron. *"Ace" Any Test.* Hawthorne, New Jersey: Career
Press, Inc., 1992. This is part of a series entitled *Ron

Fry's How to Study Program that includes *Improving Your Memory, Take Notes, Improve Your Reading, Write Papers, Manage Your Time,* and *How to Study.*

Gardner, Howard. *The Unschooled Mind: How Children Think & How Schools Should Teach.* New York: BasicBooks, HarperCollins Publisher Inc., 1991.

Gasson, Dr. I. John. *Helping Your Child Succeed at School.* Toronto: Warwick Publishing Inc., 1995.

Gasson, Dr. I. John, and Baxter, Dr. E. Paul. *Getting the Most Out of Your Child's School.* Scarborough, Ontario: McGraw-Hill Ryerson Limited, 1989.

Glasser, Dr. William. *The Quality School Teacher.* New York: HarperCollins Publishers Inc., 1993.

Highet, Gilbert. *The Art of Teaching.* Toronto: Random House of Canada Ltd., Vintage Books Edition, 1989.

Holt, John. *The Under-achieving School.* New York: Dell Publishing Co., 1969.

Kropp, Paul, and Hodson, Lynda. *The School Solution.* Toronto: Random House of Canada Limited, 1995.

Leland, Nita. *Creative Artist: A Fine Artist's Guide to Expanding Your Creativity and Achieving Your Potential.* Cincinnati, Ohio: Writer's Digest Books, 1990.

Leman, Dr. Kevin. *Growing Up Firstborn.* New York: Dell Publishing, 1989.

Lewington, Jennifer, and Orpwood, Graham. *Overdue Assignment, Taking Responsibility for Canada's Schools.* Etobicoke, Ontario: John Wiley & Sons Canada Limited, 1995.

Mandel, Harvey P., and Sander, I. Marcus. *Could Do Better, Why Children Underachieve and What to do About it.* Toronto: HarperCollins Publishers Ltd., 1995.

Martin, Michael, and Waltman-Greenwood, Cynthia. *Solve Your Child's School-related Problems.* New York: HarperCollins, 1995.

McCormack, Mark H. *What They Don't Teach You at Harvard Business School.* New York: Bantam Books, 1986.

Miller, Michael. *Dare to Live, A Guide to the Understanding of Teenage Suicide and Depression.* Pickering, Ontario: Silvio Mattacchione & Co., 1991.

Nikiforuk, Andrew. *If Learning is so Natural, Why am I going to School?* Toronto: Penguin Books, 1994.

Nikiforuk, Andrew. *School's Out.* Toronto: Macfarlane Walter & Ross, 1993.

Roberts, Wess. *Straight A's Never Made Anybody Rich.* New York: HarperCollins Publishers, 1991.

Smith, Joy. *Lies My Kid's Teacher Told Me.* Winnipeg, Manitoba: Educational Enterprises, 1995.

Steinem, Gloria. *Revolution From Within: A Book of Self-Esteem.* Toronto: Little, Brown and Company (Canada) Limited, 1992.

Magazines

Cooper, Barry. "Class Action." *Saturday Night* (September 1992).

Cusack, Veronica. "The Good School Guide." *Toronto Life* (March 1996).

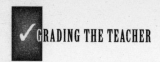

Dennis, Wendy. "Learning the hard way." *Toronto Life* (September 1993).

"Education Report '95, What Parent Power can do." *Today's Parent* (September 1995).

Fennell, Tom. "Some universities are placing new emphasis on their professors' work in the classroom." In "Special Report: Teaching Class." *Maclean's* (November 9, 1992), p. 56.

Hillerman, Anne. "Teacher, Teacher." *Mothering* (Spring Issue 1992).

Israeloff, Roberta. "Special Education Report." *Parents Magazine* (October 1992).

Owen, Gerald. "Ship of Schools, A Special Report on Education." *Homemaker's Magazine* (September 1992).

Robertson, Heather. "Deciding your child's future." *Toronto Life* (September 1992).

Newspapers

Dimerman, Sara. "A Look at Education In Toronto." *City Parent* (January 1994).

Landsberg, Michelle. "A Right-wing Attack on our Public Schools." *The Toronto Star* (September 9, 1995).

"On the Trail of the Meaning of Life." *Toronto Star* (November 28, 1992).

Straw, Jack. "Failing the Teachers." *The Times* (London) (September 20, 1990).

Weizel, Richard. "Advice for Parents on School Mysteries." *The New York Times* (November 12, 1995).

Reports

Gaskell, Dr. Jane. *Secondary Schools in Canada, The National Report of the Exemplary Schools Project*, (1995). Canadian Education Association, OISE, 252 Bloor St. W. Suite 200, Toronto, Ontario ($35.00 plus shipping).

The Ontario Ministry of Education condensed "Provincial Review Report on Alternative Schools and Programs in the Public System" (1986).

Piredda, Francesca. "Report to Parents." Ontario Ministry of Education and Training (February 1994).

The Toronto Board of Education's Fact Sheet #15 on Alternative Schools (September 1990).

The Toronto Board of Education's booklet on Alternative Elementary Schools (1989).

Video

To understand how individual differences in capabilities and assimilation of material affect the learning process, I and my friend Barbara Anthony, Hugh McMillan Rehabilitation Centre in Toronto, Ontario, highly recommend this excellent videotape workshop for both teachers and parents:

How Difficult Can This Be? Hosted by Richard D. Lavoie, $49.95 (U.S.) plus shipping and handling. To order, call 1 800 344-3337. For further information fax 703 739-5269 or write PBS Video, 1320 Braddock Place, Alexandria, Virginia, U.S.A. 22314-1698.